John Robert Shaw

Edited and with
an Introduction by
Oressa M. Teagarden

Co-editor, Jeanne L. Crabtree

Ohio University Press *Athens*

John Robert Shaw

An Autobiography of Thirty Years, 1777–1807

Library of Congress Cataloging-in-Publication Data

Shaw, John Robert, 1761-1813.
    [Life and travels of John Robert Shaw]
    John Robert Shaw : an autobiography of thirty years, 1777-1807 /
edited and with an introduction by Oressa M. Teagarden : co-editor,
Jeanne Crabtree.
        p.   cm.
    Originally published: The life and travels of John Robert Shaw.
Lexington, Ky. : D. Bradford, 1807.
    Includes bibliographical references and index.
    ISBN 0-8214-1018-0 (acid-free)
    1. Shaw, John Robert, 1761-1813. 2. United Sttates—History-
-Revolution, 1775-1783—Personal narratives. 3. Lexington (Ky.)-
-Biography. I. Teagarden, Oressa M. (Oressa Marsh), 1906-1987.
II. Crabtree, Jeanne. III. Title.
E275.S53   1992
973.3'8—dc20   91-32965
                                                            CIP

Contents

Illustrations

About the Editor

I n the early 1950s, a *Louisville* (Kentucky) *Times* feature writer and reporter, Oressa Marsh Teagarden, was shown a fragile copy of *The Life & Travels of John Robert Shaw.* This 1930 reprint of an 1807 original had been rescued from a trash pile by a research librarian, a friend of Oressa's.

As Oressa read through the yellowed pages, she became fascinated by the rapscallion Shaw and obtained permission to bring her typewriter to the library archives and copy the text of the book.

As well as a newspaper reporter, Oressa was an amateur historian of the Revolutionary and Civil War periods. Her primary interest in Shaw's autobiography was the period of history in which he lived. His misspellings and comments about his military career intrigued her. She wanted to determine the proper place names for the places Shaw had traveled to, and she wanted to correct any inaccuracies in Shaw's historical account.

For as long as Oressa remained in the Louisville area, she spent her vacations traveling Shaw's routes and documenting through extensive research the accuracy of what he wrote. After learning that the book was in the public domain, she prepared the manuscript for this book, the third publication of Shaw's autobiography, editing, researching, and footnoting it. She also wrote an introduction, which follows this essay.

From my friendship with Oressa, dating from 1965 to her death in 1987, at which time I inherited the Shaw manuscript at her bequest, it became clear to me that she was herself worthy of some exposition in this book to document her interesting life. Oressa, who preferred to be called "OT," had the misfortune to have a body that did not utilize vitamin A, and this caused premature aging. When I first came to know her, she was fifty-nine years old, and although she dressed stylishly, her white hair and heavily wrinkled visage made her look to be in her seventies. Only her petite figure, bright blue eyes, and feisty manner revealed the youthfulness of her mind and spirit.

In going through some of her writing after her death, I came across the beginning of an autobiographical sketch. She began by telling about three women named Mary who were present at her birth in 1906 in Wetzel County, West Virginia. One was Mary Earnshaw, her grandmother; another, Mary Pethtel, whom Oressa came to love, but who she could only visit surreptitiously because of a later quarrel with her grandmother; and the third, "Aunt Mary by marriage and the answer to a child's dream of feeling grown-up and important." Oressa was the last of five children born to Jefferson Davis and Ida Ash Teagarden; she was a "change-of-life" baby and unwanted. The three Marys had been told by the doctor, "Leave the baby alone—it's going to die anyway."

The tiny premature infant was nursed to health by others in the family, having been nearly abandoned by her mother. Closest to her as she was growing up were her eldest sister Arlie; her father, whom she adored; and Aunt Mary. In her adolescence, Oressa was erroneously believed to have contracted tuberculosis and was sent away to a sanatorium for treatment. Her schooling fell behind, and she was seventeen before she began high school at Hundred, West Virginia, where the Teagarden family lived. The isolation from family while at the sanatorium and the feelings of abandonment and separation from her mother could well have left the young Oressa damaged emotionally and mentally, but she was a strong and self-reliant child. Oressa's father was on her side, and when she wanted to go to college and study journalism, he agreed to pay her way.

Because she was so much younger than her brothers and sisters, it was not until her college years that she formed friendships, some of which lasted the rest of her life. By the time she received her degree in 1931 from West Virginia University, Arlie had committed the almost unpardonable sin of divorcing her husband and was living at home with their parents. Their mother was now ill and required the care of the two sisters. For the next six years, Oressa suspended her life and career to nurse her mother through her last illness.

Arlie and Oressa had a couple of things in common—both had been confined for years with ailing parents and both were at heart adventurers. While still married, Arlie and her husband had adopted the six-year-old daughter of family friends who, during the Depression, simply could not feed all of their children. Helping Arlie rear her daughter Edis was an important part of Oressa's life. Yet, Oressa said that she never wanted children of her own because she feared she would transmit her own feelings of abandonment to any child she might have.

After their mother's death, the two sisters hitchhiked from Hundred to Louisville, Kentucky. First living in boarding houses until they found work and later buying a house, they bound their lives together. Oressa got a job with the *Louisville Courier-Journal* and Arlie hired out as a practical nurse. They shared the care of Arlie's daughter. For the *Courier-Journal*

Oressa wrote special feature articles, her genre for the rest of her working life. In 1942 she began a long association with the *Louisville Times*, writing for the magazine section and as its drama critic. She also served the *Times* as an editor, picture editor, columnist, and feature writer.

During her eighteen years at the *Times*, she interviewed the famous and the infamous. She was sent to New York to review new shows and was courted by those who needed the influence of critics. Interspersed with the exciting times of her career were the periods when she was responsible for the care and guidance of her niece while Arlie traveled with wealthy older people seeking a change of environment to restore their health.

Oressa's independent lifestyle led some of her relatives to wonder if she might be lesbian. However, in her late twenties, Oressa had been deeply in love with a man who died from lung cancer before they could marry. Later she had a long-standing affair with a divorced man that never came to marriage because he maintained close contact with his former wife and their children. After this affair ended, Oressa socialized with other eligible men but never considered marrying any of them. This may have been partly because the premature aging she suffered became evident during these years, and she began to look much older than she was.

Infighting among the management of the *Times* caused great unhappiness for Oressa, and in 1956 the sisters moved to Boise, Idaho, for three years and then to Norman, Oklahoma. In both cities, Oressa continued her newspaper career. Her last job was with the *Norman Transcript* as feature writer and copy editor until her retirement in 1967.

It was about 1956 that Oressa and Arlie began making trips to Mexico, usually with Monterrey as their base. They came to know a young bellboy. As the years went by, the bellboy grew up, married, and fathered ten children. Oressa was godmother to most of these children, and for as long as she could afford it, she sent them gifts at Christmas. Clearly, this woman who did not want children of her own demonstrated that she could have been a loving mother.

When Arlie, eighteen years older than Oressa, became very ill and senile, Oressa finally had to put her sister in a nursing home. Oressa visited each day, especially at mealtimes, trying to coax Arlie to eat. But now Oressa herself was experiencing the painful effects of osteoporosis, which would worsen to the end of her life at age eighty.

Our friendship began when I went to work in the newsroom of the *Norman Transcript* in 1965. Only a few of the newsroom people liked Oressa. Most thought she was too old to be still working (she wasn't, she just looked much older than she was), or they felt that as copy editor of their work, she was too critical. As we became better acquainted, my husband and I were invited to Oressa and Arlie's home for a Christmas party and thereafter began to know more about this fascinating woman and her life. After Oressa left the *Transcript* and began to devote herself to caring for Arlie, we would have the two to our home on holidays. Oressa came to know our children, never forgetting their birthdays, their ages, and later their wedding days and the dates our grandchildren were born.

For a number of years after she retired from journalism, Oressa worked freelance preparing book indexes. She also did proofreading for the *American Journal of Botany*. Finally, the intense effort of coping with the pain of osteoporosis and numerous hospitalizations forced her to give up all work. The last few years of her life were spent worrying that she, like Arlie, would become senile. She begged not to be put in a nursing home as long as she was in her right mind, which, of course, we honored.

Generous but demanding accountability, intelligent but always willing to share what she knew, feisty and witty, when

Oressa died quietly in her own home on July 19, 1987, she left a void that cannot be filled. A lot of her life went into researching John Robert Shaw, who became almost a contemporary to her. Her research has kept the memory of John Robert Shaw alive. I hope that this essay will do the same for her.

Jeanne L. Crabtree

Acknowledgements

The list of acknowledgements prepared by editor Oressa M. Teagarden is now, in 1990, aged by more than twenty years. It would, however, be important to her to have it included in this volume. After all these years, it is understandable if many of the persons whose assistance she recognized are no longer at the positions named, or even some are deceased. It is hoped that if any readers know these persons or their descendants, the acknowledgement of their assistance will be called to their attention. —J.C.

This autobiography perhaps would emerge as the tall tales of an adventurer if it were presented now, after 162 years [now 183 years], without research into the life and times of the author. For assistance in this research I am indebted to a number of persons and organizations. Foremost among these is Ellen Harding, former research librarian at the Louisville Free Public Library, Kentucky, for making the remaining fragile copy of the autobiography available to me and for identifying George L. Fowler, from whose edition this reprint is presented. My thanks go also to Ludie J. Kincead at the Filson Club, Louisville, Kentucky, for genealogical data and eighteenth-century Kentucky place names; to R.E. Simmermacher, meteorologist at the Wilkes Barre Scranton Airport Weather Bureau and to R.W. Schloemer, deputy director of climatology, Environmental Science Services Administration, Silver Springs, Maryland; and to the president of the Wyoming Historical Society, Wilkes Barre, for information on early weather accounts in Pennsylvania. In addition, thanks to David C. Munn, reference librarian, State Library, Trenton, New Jersey, for the account of the Old Tappan massacre; to Ethel L. Hutchins, History and Literature Department, Public Library of Cincinnati and Hamilton County, for defining the boundaries of Fort Washington and for accounts of Shaw's well drilling in Cincinnati; to H. Dorothy English, Pennsylvania Room, Carnegie Library of Pittsburgh, for information about Fort McIntosh and early Pittsburgh; and to the librarian, Army War College, Carlisle Barracks, Pennsylvania.

To Jeanne H. Mahler, Public Documents Department, Free Library of Philadelphia, for early place names and pension laws; to Laura G. Lundgren, Lancaster County (Pennsylvania) Historical Society, for maps and other information on Lancaster County; to Mary Kate Akkola, Norman Free Library, for assistance in locating needed information; to the University of Oklahoma Army ROTC unit, Norman, Oklahoma, for assistance in clarifying matters of military procedure and laws; to the Greater Carlisle Area Chamber of Commerce, for maps and early history of Carlisle and Cumberland County; to the South Carolina Department of Archives and History, Columbia, concerning military campaigns of the South; to the Historical Society of Montgomery County, Pennsylvania, and of Delaware

County, for early regional data; and to the Virginia State Library for information on Colonel Baylor and his cavalry regiment at Old Tappan, New Jersey.

Last, my gratitude to Jeanne Crabtree and Doris Morris, my friends, whose advice and encouragement have helped to make this volume possible.

OT

The Wonderful recovery of JOHN R. SHAW

I'll praife the LORD while I have breath,
    And fhout his holy name,
And all the wonders of his works
    I loudly will proclaim.

Introduction

In 1791, the eccentric genius, John Robert
Shaw, the well digger, was at Fort Washington
where "I dug the first well that ever was in
Cincinnati."

— Greve's *Centennial History of Cincinnati*

J ohn Robert Shaw had been blown up. While recuperating
from this mishap, the eighteenth-century soldier, Lo-
thario, and well digger for the army and the new settle-
ments had ample time to reflect on what he chose to call his
"misspent life."

While still a teenager, Shaw had come to Rhode Island as a
British redcoat to be a "gentleman soldier" for the king. After
some chicaneries as an escaped prisoner of war (he even joined
the rebel army), after posing as witch doctor and fortune teller,
after traveling about as a begging veteran and being almost
frozen in General Harmer's American First army, Shaw came to
Kentucky late in the fall of 1791. All the while, he said, he "took
many a delectable frolic with the bottle and venturesome turn
with the ladies."

Despite Christian fortitude and quack doctors, "bottle
fever" plagued Shaw all of his days, even while he was engaged
in the dangerous business of blasting wells and quarrying stone.
His "bottle fever" no doubt accounted for the carelessness that

resulted in his being injured in explosions four times. These were not his only accidents. So numerous were his bizarre wounds that he was called "Lexington's most tragic figure." After one accident, his physician, Dr. James Fishback, took note of Shaw's shortcomings as well as his better qualities when he described his patient's multiple wounds in an article for publication in the *Kentucky Gazette* in Lexington:

> John Robert Shaw, whose melancholy condition is the subject of this narrative, is a well digger and stone quarrier by trade, and is not less distinguished for his honesty, industry and usefulness, than for his accumulated evils (if such they may be called) which have pursued him for many years past.

Shaw, who often advertised in the *Gazette*,[1] inserted the following notice in the newspaper on November 27, 1806, during his convalescence: "In a few weeks I shall present to the public a narrative of 30 years of my life and travels, five different times a soldier, three times shipwrecked, 12 months a prisoner of war, and four times blown up." In the summer of 1807, Shaw's book was printed by Daniel Bradford in Lexington,[2] titled *The Life and Travels of John Robert Shaw: A Narrative of the Life and Travels of the Well-Digger, now resident of Lexington, Kentucky, Written by Himself.*[3]

The costs of publishing the autobiography were borne by more than a thousand subscribers from New England to Tennessee. (See Appendix.) Most of them, however, were from Pennsylvania and Kentucky, where the ebullient Englishman was a familiar figure in almost every settlement. The list of subscribers reads like a who's who of post–revolutionary war history: Christopher Greenup, governor of Kentucky; Henry Clay; Simon Kenton; Judge John Rowan; and many others of prominence.

His subscribers must have taken with a grain of salt—as we

should now—Shaw's declaration that he was "almost totally illiterate," for in the style of the eighteenth-century narrative, he offered a lively view of the American scene over a period of three decades following independence.

Shaw, keenly aware of his own shortcomings, was unassuming, modest, and sympathetic. Often taken advantage of and sometimes harshly treated, he never repaid such treatment in kind. On the other hand, generous and faithful friends came often to his assistance in adversities. To these he freely expressed his gratitude. Shaw was equally at ease with the lowly and the great. On crutches, he pleaded his case for a soldier's pension before the Pennsylvania Assembly in 1785 and won a promise from the assembly and later from General Henry Knox, secretary of war, that the pension laws would be amended at the next session to include the ineligible cases such as his. The amendment came, as promised, in 1787, and the law was further strengthened in 1789.[4] Shaw, however, did not apply again for a pension.

Shaw wrote without reservation about the people he met, the places he saw, and his own intemperance. He described battles and incidents of the American Revolution as he, a common soldier, saw them. As a seventeen-year-old, he saw the Tappan Massacre (his youth may account for his exaggerated view), and he witnessed some of the foolish miscalculations made by both sides in the conflict. One that occurred after the battle of Camden on August 16, 1780, gave the well digger a chuckle. General Thomas Sumter, retreating with a number of Tory prisoners, a hogshead of rum, and some captured English provisions, had halted too early in his flight to pick peaches in a South Carolina orchard and to ration the captured liquor, only to be surprised there by the pursuing enemy.

Shaw also described how the American soldiers tarried at Stony Point after the siege while a British unit just across the Hudson River at Verplanck's Point watched them and expected an attack at any moment. "But the Yankee army lay in our front eating molasses instead of attacking us." British blunders were common too. On one occasion during the campaigns in the South, Shaw's unit camped near a Moravian town because it was said to be sympathetic to the Crown.

> The inhabitants were very generous in rolling out their whiskey barrels to make us drunk. . . . And, I believe, had the Americans been vigilant, they would have succeeded in their insidious design, for it is my opinion that there were not fifty sober men among us.

Among the reasons Shaw stated for writing his autobiography was his desire to warn young people against following his example. At the turn of the nineteenth century, Shaw was caught in the maelstrom of religious dissension that was rife in Kentucky. Having turned to religion to cure his drinking habit, he joined the Methodists. "But alas!" he declared. "Religious controversies began to disseminate in this the dawning of my spiritual salvation, which caused the backsliding of a number, with myself."

Camp meetings in the woods lasted all day and long into the night. To these meetings came many people of different tenets and denominations to hear speakers who often purveyed strange doctrines. Shaw struck back bitterly at the controversialists, whom he believed to be, in part at least, responsible for his own inability to replace vice with virtue.

He concluded that the young should be warned "against the pitfalls of sin" that had caused him to lead a "misspent life." Except for his closing paragraphs, the lengthy address on his religious soundings that failed him has been omitted here from the otherwise delightful account of the adventures of John Robert Shaw.

After the distribution of his autobiography, the well digger vanished from the historical record except for his continuing advertisements about his work, some of which are reproduced here, and his obituary. Six years after the autobiography appeared, on August 30, 1813, Shaw was killed in his fifth explosives accident. The *Lexington Reporter,* a weekly newspaper, carried an account of his death in its issue of Saturday, September 14, 1813: "John Robert Shaw died on Monday last, of an accidental gunpowder explosion at the bottom of the well of Robert Wilson. He was an honest, industrious citizen of Lexington for twenty years." Shaw's burial place is not known, but it is likely to have been in a cemetery on Lexington's Main Street just west of Spring Street, or in a churchyard at Walnut and Short streets. Both were in the heart of the city, and tall buildings now cover the sites.

Almost a century passed after Shaw's narrative was published before any historians remembered Shaw and his memoirs. In 1882, Robert Peter in his *History of Fayette County* offered this brief biographical account:

> John Robert Shaw, the well digger, the most eccentric and unfortunate character known to early Lexington, died in the summer of 1814 [1813]. He commenced life as a British soldier, and served with the troops sent against the rebellious American colonies, but fought on both sides before he got through, and afterward participated in the Indian campaigns of Harmer and St. Clair.
>
> He settled in Lexington in 1791, having come from Fort Washington, as Cincinnati was then called, was married by Rev. Toulmin to a humble protege of Col. Robertson, and soon at-

tained a curious notoriety as a well digger, a prophetic water
wizard, a see-er of visions, and for his misfortunes, sufferings,
and remarkable escapes from death, which left him a scarred and
dilapidated cripple.

In 1930, George L. Fowler, a Louisvillian, again printed
the Shaw autobiography. Fowler did not explain how or where
he got the original version. The limited copies of this reprint
have almost disappeared [at this writing in the early 1970s].
There are three known copies in the files of public libraries.
Perhaps some are treasured by collectors.

Fowler left the impression in his introduction that the
reprint, which bore no copyright, was primarily for the purpose
of preserving the narrative.

> After the passing of a period of Victorianism that would have
> disdained him without reservation, [Shaw's] oblivion was com-
> plete. . . . Some day this narrative of a well digger will keep
> company with the other autobiographies of lovable rascals that
> enjoy the twofold desideratum of a book, not only to survive, but
> also to be read.
>
> If this edition shall in any way hasten the recognition of the
> most significant contribution the early west has to offer to Amer-
> ican letters, I shall be content.

Shaw's story presented here follows the reprint by Fowler.
To this have been added notes of explanation and verification
provided by the editor's research. Punctuation, capitalization,
misspellings, and an occasional awkward construction have
been retained. Inconsistencies in spelling also occur, as do
some obsolete words. Shaw used both British and American
spellings of such words as *color, honor,* and *favor.*

Frequently military titles preceding names are not capitalized, and the ranks of officers of national repute sometimes

appear incorrectly. *Christian* is usually written with a lowercase *c*, whereas *Quaker, Moravian* and the like are capitalized most of the time.

Misspelled names may be noted in the list of Shaw's subscribers. Since it would be impossible to check the spellings of all the names, they have been transcribed here as Shaw wrote them.

Oressa M. Teagarden, 1971

Chapter 1

"I'll show you a place where the streets are paved with pancakes."

I was born on the 19th day of August, 1761, in the town of Manningham, in the parish of Bradford, Yorkshire, Old England.[1] My father was by occupation a stuff weaver, and I was put to the same business at the age of 12 years.

About two years after, I unfortunately formed an acquaintance with a certain Thomas Fields, who used every artifice and device in his power to draw me into vicious company, in order to bring me to ruin, which he too easily effected.

The first "great adventure" in which he engaged me was this: having learned of me that a certain old gentleman, with whom my father was particularly intimate, was in good circumstances, and had always money at command, he addressed me as follows:

"Now, John," says he, "let us go and borrow some money of this man in your father's name."

Accordingly through a long persuasion he prevailed upon me, and putting a plausible story in my mouth, off we went, and borrowed two shillings (sterling).

Being as yet a novice in wickedness, and altogether un-practiced in the profligate ways of the town, I was entirely at a loss, how to dispose of my ill-gotten treasure. But friend Tom soon found the way to the tavern, where to my shame I got drunk for the first time.

"Well, Tom," said I, having somewhat recovered my senses, "what is to be done now? My father, it seems, has discovered my roguery—there he comes."

Poor Tom made no reply, but slipped out the back door like a thief and left me to answer for my misconduct to my father, who led me off by the shoulder like a criminal. This broke the way for my total overthrow.

My next offense was sabbath breaking, to which my father was much opposed, being a strict churchman, and called by his neighbors a sober, moral man.

But as one bad practice generally brings on another, the blush of innocence being worn off, I soon transgressed again, which induced me to apply to my old friend Tom and other new comrades, for advice what to do to avoid the effects of my father's displeasure.

Upon this, Tom and Jack immediately proposed that we should all go and enlist for soldiers, get clear of work, and be gentlemen at once. So we all concluded to go and enlist the first opportunity that offered. And lest this should come to my father's ears and I should thus be prevented from accomplishing my design, I determined to lose no time.

Accordingly in a few days I made my escape to a place called Leeds, a considerable town in the west Riding of Yorkshire, and 10 miles from my father's house, where I hoped to be secure and spend my hours more agreeably. But the keeping of bad company is a growing evil, by which my situation was rendered so unpleasant that I began to entertain serious thoughts of returning home, having found by experience that my uncle John Hall's house was not my home. Accordingly I returned to my father, like the repenting prodigal, and lived with him contentedly for some time.

But as old habits are hard to be relenquished, I again relapsed into my former irregularities and grew weary of labor. In 1777 I ran away a second time, being, as I fancied, ill-treated by my stepmother. Though the true motive for my elopement was this: Early on Monday morning my father went to Bailden mill. He told me before he set off that if I did not finish my last week's work, when he came home he would give me a trimming. This being too hard a task, I put on my best apparel and directed my course to Shipley and thence to Windal to a magician to have my fortune told.

After that I pursued my journey to Coverly; and on Coverly moor I seriously deliberated with myself what was best to be done. At first I thought of returning home again, but the dread of paternal chastisement and the ridicule of my acquaintances, to which I must be exposed in case I came back the second time, banished all thoughts of domestic concerns and firmly fixed my resolution of enlisting as a king's soldier.

So on I went to the place of destination and arrived there late in the evening. No sooner had I entered the town than, to my great joy, I met one of the 33d regiment's recruits, who, when I told him my business, gladly gave me his hand and said,

"Come, my fine lad, the king wants soldiers. Come on, my fine boy, I'll show you a place where the streets are paved with pancakes and where the hogs are going through the streets carrying knives and forks on their backs and crying 'Who will come and eat?' "

I accompanied him to the recruiting party's place of rendezvous, at the Sign of the Leopard, behind the Shambles in Bridget Street, and was introduced to the recruiting sergeant, whose name was James Shackleton, and also to the corporal, whose name was Goggell.

Says the sergeant, "Well, my fine lad, will you enlist for a soldier? Where did you come from?"

"I came from Bailden."

"What is your name?"

"My name is John Robert Shaw."

"Are you willing to serve the king?"

"Yes, sir."

"Well, here is a shilling to serve King George III in the honorable 33d regiment of foot, commanded by the honorable Lord Cornwallis, knight and baronet of the star and garter. Well, my lad, you must go to the captain."

So we went to the captain. Says the sergeant, "Here is a young lad who wishes to enlist for a soldier."

"Well, my lad," says the captain, "how old are you?"

"Fifteen or sixteen." [2]

"[W]ell, sergeant, bring the standard."

It was brought, and I measured five feet and one inch, without my shoes.

"Well, my lad," says the captain, "you are too low and under size and I cannot take you. But here is a shilling and I'll give you a new hat and a cockade and a new suit of clothes, and go home and be a good boy and go to school and come to me two or three years hence and I will enlist you."

The name of this generous captain was Carr.

"No," said I, "if you will not take me, I will go and enlist for a drummer in the 59th regiment." For recruits were being taken in at Leeds to fill up that regiment which had been cut off at the battle of Bunker Hill.

"Well, then," said the captain, "since the lad is determined to be a soldier, and appears to be a promising youth, I will take him. Here are three guineas and a crown to drink His Majesty's health. Now my fine lad, be a good boy and I will take you to be my waiter. Sergeant Shackleton, you must take this young soldier under your care, and provide a billet for him, and get him good quarters. And tomorrow go with him to buy such necessities as you think he will stand in need of to make him appear like a gentleman."

"Come on, my fine Bailden lad," says the sergeant. "Come to my quarters." And when I arrived there among my jolly companions, "Drummer, beat the point of war," was the word. For which a crown bowl of punch was called for to drink His Majesty's health. So we spent that night merrily and all retired to bed at 12 o'clock.

I was put to bed to a naked man, which I thought strange. But this is a common custom with soldiers in order to save their linens, as it is the policy of soldiers to preserve their clothing; for we had to appear three times a day dressed and powdered.

Meanwhile, my absence occasioned a great deal of concern in my father's family, and much solicitude to know what was become of me. It was at length learned that I had gone to enlist for a soldier at Leeds. About two weeks after my elopement my father accompanied by my uncle set out in search of me, and having arrived at the place of rendezvous, inquired for me of the sergeant.

"Would you know your son if you saw him?" said the sergeant.

My father answered in the affirmative.

The reader will please to observe that at the time I was then setting between my father and uncle.

"What is your son's name?" asked the sergeant.

"His name is John Robert Shaw from Bailden."

"Well, there he sits between you."

As soon as my father had composed himself, he proposed to me to be bought off and return home, but I obstinately refused it and replied, "If you buy me off today, I will enlist tomorrow for a drummer."

Here I cannot avoid reflecting on the shamefulness of my

conduct; and among the numerous errors and improprieties of which I have been guilty this must be considered as none of the least. Ingratitude—that blackest of vices—steels the heart against all noble and exalted emotions and obliterates the finest feelings of the soul.

But to proceed with my narrative—my father finding me inflexibly determined to continue in the army, gave over all entreaties and departed in tears, leaving me to pursue the bent of my inclinations; for my situation, surrounded by giddy, thoughtless wretches like myself, effectually precluded all serious reflection on the improprieties of my conduct.

The next day I was sent with a billet to the Sign of the Cross-keys on Quarry Hill and there treated like a gentleman.

In a few weeks, however, the militia was called to do duty in the town of Leeds, and all the recruiting parties of the different regiments were to be billeted out in the country villages. It fell my lot to go to Bromley, from which once a day I was obliged to go to Leeds in order to march around with the recruiting party and exercise myself in running, jumping and learning to walk straight.

One evening as I was returning to my quarters, having rashly attempted to leap over a fence, I stuck a tenter hook in my leg, which so lacerated the same that I was obliged to hobble back to town as well as I could, where a surgeon was called in to dress the wound. I was then billeted at the Sign of the Eagle and Child in Cawe Lane and there treated very well. But not being satisfied, I was sent to the hospital at the upper end of the town, where having remained for eight weeks, I was discharged by the surgeon and sent with a billet to my old quarters at the Sign of the Cross-Keys on Quarry Hill.

After some time I obtained a furlough for eight weeks to go home to Bailden to visit my father. During this period I became acquainted with one Samuel Crabtree, an old soldier and lately from Minorca. From this man I received great encouragement concerning the military life, and was highly delighted on hearing him recount the particulars of the many sieges and battles in which he had been engaged.

While at Bailden I had frequent visits from several of my relatives and neighbors, all endeavoring to persuade me to be bought off and abandon the army. All their arguments and expostulations were in vain, though my grandfather, who was in tolerable circumstances and willing to assist me in case of good behavior, repeatedly declared that if I persisted in my contumacy, he would leave me only a shilling to buy a halter, as no better fate could be expected by such a graceless and undutiful youth. Yet, regardless of consequences, my resolution remained unshaken. Still I was determined to be a "gentleman soldier."

The term of my furlough being expired, I returned to the recruiting party at Leeds, and was received with expressions of great applause for my constancy.

We afterwards spent a considerable time in recruiting at the country villages, and with a good deal of success. While thus employed we had an account of the battle of Long Island, and of the gallant and soldier-like behavior of the 33d regiment, commanded by Lieutenant Colonel William Webster, for which, as a mark of distinction an additional riband[3] of the orange colour was bestowed: the whole consisting of the red, blue, white and yellow. These colours composed our cockade. Four guineas more were given as a bounty to each recruit, which, with the 3 guineas and a crown, which they received at the time of enlisting, as already mentioned, amounted to seven guineas and a crown.

Shortly after, having gained a sufficient number of recruits, we received orders to march. Accordingly, we marched on through Wakefield, Blackbarnsley, Sheffield, Northampton, Nottingham, and so on to London.

We halted a few days in London in order to take some

refreshments, for there was a Yorkshire man in the city, who made it a constant rule to treat all the Yorkshire recruits enlisted for the 33d regiment, having himself been an old soldier, and served the king in that regiment formerly in Flanders. So we all ate and drank heartily, and parted with our generous host in high spirits, and marched on to Greenwich, about five miles east from London, where we remained for three days, and viewed the curiosities of the place.

Among these nothing so much engaged my attention and commanded my admiration as the Royal Hospital. It was formerly a royal palace, built by Humphrey, duke of Gloucester, enlarged by Henry VII, and completed by Henry VIII. The later often made this his place of residence, as also did the queens, Mary and Elizabeth, who were born in it. It was greatly improved and embellished by Charles II, who spent 36,000 pounds on that part of it which is now the first wing of the hospital toward London.

King William III, in 1694, granted it, "with nine acres of ground thereto belonging, to be converted into a royal hospital for old and disabled seamen, the widows and children of those who lost their lives in the service, and for the encouragement of navigation." Upwards of 2,000 old disabled seamen are maintained in this hospital—they are vulgarly called the king's beef eaters. The buildings are undoubtedly the finest in the world.

From Greenwich there is a fine view of the city of London, and the Thames with the shipping of almost all nations.—The royal observatory commands a most delightful prospect—charming indeed beyond description.

Having spent our limited time in amusing ourselves with the curiosities of the place, we marched on to Chatham barracks, the finest garrison in old England. Chatham is the principal station of the royal navy and the yards and magazines are furnished with all sorts of naval stores, as well as materials for building the largest ships of war. Here are at least 1,000 ship carpenters working every day.—They work 12 hours in a day, i. e., from 6 o'clock in the morning until 6 in the evening. Everything here is conducted with the utmost regularity.

We were now in barrack quarters, 16 or 20 privates in a room, with a sergeant to keep good order, and purchase provisions, and see it divided, when cooked and prepared according to the laws of the place.

Four pence a day for each private soldier are laid out for provisions at market; a half-penny to the doctor; the same to the chaplain and a penny for clothing; the whole pay of a soldier being six pence per day, with the queen's bounty of 19 shillings a year, and a complete suit of clothes consisting of 1 hat, 1 vest, 1 pair of breeches, 1 shirt, 1 pair of shoes, 1 pair of stockings, and 1 stock and stock buckle.

While we lay at Chatham, we were constantly exercising and learning the military evolutions under corporal Coggell, whose experience and skill in such matters were equalled by few in the army. There were 19 in number in the 33d regiment, who after only six months practice, challenged the whole garrison to contend with them in military discipline.

The garrison then consisted of 80 additional companies, besides the first regiment of the Royal Scotch, (as they were called) who had been in practice for many years.

A review of clothing was then and probably yet in practice every Monday morning: each soldier on the parade, with his knapsack on his back, and his firelock and accoutrements in complete order—drums beating and colours flying; and to crown the whole the instrument called the cat and nine tails[4] tipt with brass wire and constantly displayed. The review being ended, if any clothing is missing, a circle is formed, and a drumhead court martial is called and the delinquent is tried and punished according to his desert.

After lying in Chatham barracks almost a year, a draught was made, and four hundred of us deluded out under the pretense of doing duty at Portsmouth. The next morning a sergeant was dispatched to prepare the barracks, as we supposed, for our reception. We accordingly marched on to Portsmouth in good spirits, hoping to spend a few happy years in that place.

But how great was our disappointment when we arrived at Portsmouth and found the streets lined with old pensioners to guard us safe on board a ship! The boats were ready to convey us all on board of the ship *None-such*, which then lay at anchor in the port.—The cries and lamentations of the poor, raw country soldiers were sufficient to have excited the compassion in the breast of the rudest barbarians; and, as for myself, I thought I was going to the Devil, when they rolled us down the hatchways like so much lumber.

Having each received some bedding and an allowance of provisions, we lay promiscuously, and crowded together in the utmost confusion. The next day we weighed anchor and sailed for the Isle of Wight, where we lay four weeks; after which we set sail for Ireland, favoured at first with a pleasant breeze; but we had not been sailing more than 12 hours, before we were surprised with a thunderstorm and a contrary wind.

It was, I think, about 11 O'clock at night, when a man on the forecastle espied a rock, close ahead of the ship; upon which he called out to the steerman at the helm, "about ship;" which was done with all possible speed and so by the skill and dexterity of the mariners & the mercy of Providence, we were preserved from being wrecked on the rocks of Scilly.

Thus extricated from danger, we proceeded on our voyage and soon anchored in the harbour called the Cove of Cork, which is perhaps the most spacious and commodius haven in the world. The entrance is safe, and the whole navy of England might ride in it, secure from every wind that blows. Ships from England, bound for all parts of the West Indies, take in here a great deal of their provisions; and for the same purpose the Cove of Cork is visited by the vessels of many other nations.

Ships of burthen, however, are obliged to unload at a place called Passage, five miles and a half from the city, the channel not admitting vessels of above 150 tons.—This port we entered in the beginning of February, 1778, and were all separated and put on board of different vessels.

It fell my lot to go on board the *Alexandria* of 24 gune;—and she was called "a letter of marque." There were 19 Englishmen and six Irishmen who were brought on board in irons, and 24 Hessians, making in all 49 in number, to do duty as marines. Our ship's crew consisted of 60 able-bodied seamen, besides officers, one captain, 1st, 2nd, and 3d mates, one boatswain, one carpenter and a cook and cook's mate.

A fleet of transports then lay in the Cove of Kinsale repairing their rigging, and embarking provisions for America. Kinsale, especially in time of war, is a place of much business, and frequented by rich, homeward bound fleets, as also by ships of war. The cove is a convenient and beautiful harbour, and lies about seven miles from the city of Cork.

The town is defended by a strong fort called Charles's Fort; and on the opposite shore there are two villages called Cove and Scilly; the inhabitants of which are generally native Irish and live in low built houses, made of mud, on a beautiful eminence, ranging with the barracks, and facing the inlet of the harbour. The barracks are capable of lodging and containing 12 companies of foot, besides a regiment at Charles's Fort. The garrison, however, then consisted of only four companies, with 16 or 20 pieces of cannon, and deemed sufficient to protect the town and harbour.

We lay eight weeks on board before we were ready to sail, during which time we were visited by the bomb ketches, in order to sell and buy all sorts of necessities; for we had no liberty

to go on shore, except two men at a time. We weighed anchor
April 7th in company with upwards of 20 transports, (besides
two letters of marque) laden with provisions, as well as men to
assist in carrying on the unjust and unhappy war against the
American colonies.

We met with nothing extraordinary during the voyage;
only we were born off our course on the roads of certain islands,
which I think belonged to Portugal, where we got in exchange
for such necessities as we could spare, oranges, coconuts and
pineapples. Continuing our voyage from thence, we arrived
safely in America, and landed on Rhode Island, in the space of
three months from the time of our setting sail from the coast of
Ireland.

We remained on Rhode Island doing duty, while the British army were on their march from Philadelphia.

I joined the 33d regiment on Long Island at Graves-end[5];
and then we marched to Bedford, [New York], where we lay
until the beginning of autumn, when a detachment was called
out to perform, as we supposed, some great exploit. This
detachment consisted of the 33d and 42nd regiments, with two
companies of the body guards, commanded by the colonels
Webster and Frazer. We went on board the flat bottomed boats
just as it began to grow dark, and pursued our expedition, and
landed on the beach about four miles from Elizabethtown
point,[6] with our pilot, or guide, as we thought.

We had marched a mile through the marsh before we
discovered the trick;—our pilot had left us in the snare; sometimes up to the middle in mud and water; sometimes over head
and ears in the ditches, crawling over one another in the greatest confusion.

At length with much difficulty we made our appearance
near Elizabethtown just at daybreak, in woeful pickle, all be-
daubed with mud and mire, as black as chimney sweepers; we
looked more like frightening the people of the town than

The ship *None-such* in distress on the coast of Sicily. [Scilly. Ed.]

making them run for fear of the sword and bayonet. In this plight we advanced up to the town and took it.

And as a further instance of British inhumanity, the barracks were set on fire and burnt down with about ten or twelve poor sick soldiers in them.

This being the day the continental troops were to draw their provisions, the English officers called on the bakers for their bread, but the bakers very boldly answered: "this bread is for gentlemen and not for you d----d bloody backs." Bread was therefore taken by force.

We then marched on to form a line between the river and the town, leaving two companies for a rear guard; but the Americans being reenforced with 4,000 troops, got between us and the river; now who dare say the English never turned their backs, or fled from an enemy?—Colonel Webster was, it is true, for charging on the enemy, but Colonel Frazer, who was the oldest officer, and had the command, gave orders to face to the right, and make the best of our way to the boats.

That moment the enemy fired with their artillery, and killed two men of Captain Campbell's company, of the 33d regiment, whose names were Proctor and Keith; and according to our colonel's account, these men "died in glory." And so, pursuant to our orders, we took to our heels and made our way to the boats in the utmost disorder.

The bakers of Elizabethtown had now the satisfaction of seeing the English scattering and leaving behind them the bread which they had forcibly taken away at the point of a bayonet. On this occasion, we had two killed, as already mentioned, two wounded, and five taken prisoner; besides a considerable number wounded as we made our escape from the East River.

We hurried down with all possible speed, landed at Brooklyn ferry opposite to New York, and proceeded on to Bedford and lay there for some time.

Chapter 2

"I will eat my dinner [tomorrow] in Camden or in hell."

—General Horatio Gates

Not long after, an army was called forth to go on an expedition up the East River. We all embarked and sailed some distance above Bedford, where we landed, marched to the town, plundered and burned it, with all the shipping in the harbour. Such predatory excursions, of which this is but a small specimen, reflect dishonor on the British name, and consign the reputation of the British officers who conducted them to eternal infamy.

The next day we marched into the country without opposition, except for a few of the militia who brought on a skirmish; but they were soon dispersed, and we proceeded on our march without further interruption. In this excursion, among other plunder, we took a store of molasses, the hogsheads being rolled out and their heads knocked in, a soldier's wife went to dip her camp kettle in a hogshead of molasses, and while she was stooping in order to fill her kettle, a soldier slipped behind her and threw her into the hogshead; when she was hauled out, a bystander then threw a parcel of feathers on her, which

adhering to the molasses made her appear frightful enough;—
This little circumstance afforded us a good deal of amusement.

We then returned to our ships, well satisfied with our
booty, and soon arrived at our former quarters on Long Island.

A few weeks after this, a most inhuman massacre took
place near Tappan in New Jersey.[1]—A farmer and his son living
near each other, it happened that a small regiment of light horse
(raised a short time before in Virginia and known by the name of
Lady Washington's regiment) quartered at their houses and
barns in number about 300; the son being a true born American
and the father a detestable tory; the latter went to New York and
gave information of those unhappy soldiers, and offered to lead
us to the place where they lay.

Accordingly General Grey undertook the barbarous task,
and ordered out 1,000 troops, marching them one half to the
right and the other to the left, with this hard-hearted tory and
one of his associates to pilot us to the unhappy spot, where the
shocking scene commenced.

When the advanced guard came up to the yard gate, the
sentry was asleep. One of the officers of the grenadiers instantly
cut off his head, without a word. The 33d regiment, to which I
belonged, was about three miles off when the cruel carnage
began; but as we approached, the shrieks and screams of the
hapless victims whom our savage fellow soldiers were butcher-
ing, were sufficient to have melted into compassion the heart of
a Turk or a Tartar.—

Tongue cannot tell nor pen unfold the horrors of that
dismal night.—Some were seen having their arms cut off, and
others with their bowels hanging out crying for mercy.—

To preserve, however, some appearance of clemency, 43
were admitted prisoners of war; seven of the whole regiment,
being out reconnoitering, escaped. The killed and wounded
amounted to 250.—How destitute of natural affection must

have been the heart of the father, who could invite an enemy to murder his own son in cold blood! And how contrary to the principles of honor it was in the enemy to accept such invitation! Let Britain boast no more of her honour, her science and civilization; but with shame hide her head in the dust; her fame is gone; Tappan will witness against her.—Having performed this ignoble exploit, the few prisoners that were spared being conducted to New York by a guard of British soldiers, and the wounded sent off in wagons, we returned to Long Island to be ready for another scene of British barbarity.

In 1779 we marched up the North River[2] to Verplanck's Neck, commonly called the King's ferry. There was a bomb-proofed blockhouse in the fort, which mounted two six-pounders opposite to Stony Point. The fort at Verplanck's stood on the east side of the river, where were stationed the 33d regiment, colonel Robertson's corps, colonel Fannen's corps, and major Ferguson's rifle company, making in all about 700 rank and file, able-bodied fighting men, commanded by lieutenant colonel Webster.

We formed a blockhouse one mile from the fort, on a piece of rising ground.—This blockhouse mounted two three-pounders, and was well set with pickets, and commanded by one captain, one lieutenant, one ensign, two sergeants, four corporals, with a drummer and fifer, and fifty private soldiers, with a picket 100 yards in front, the guard consisting of one sergeant, one corporal and twelve privates, forming a line of four sentinels.

When this was completed, a range of batteries were erected, with two blockhouses, one on the right and the other on the left side of the batteries, so as to command both the land and the river. These works mounted six six-pounders and one long 18-pounder, with a great deal of swivels. There was a deep ditch in front of the works with three rows of abatis 40 yards apart, and three large piles of tar barrels between the rows of abatis, where stood a man with a slow match ready to set fire at the approach of the enemy.

During the building of these fortifications, the regulation was, one half on duty and the other on fatigue. While we continued there, which was nearly four months, we generally lay at night with our accoutrements on and with our firelocks in our arms.

Stony Point was a strong post on the west side of the river, nearly opposite to Verplanck's. The works had been completed and repaired with the utmost assiduity; so that they were now in a very strong state of defense, and were garrisoned by the 17th regiment of foot, one company of the 71st regiment of grenadiers, and a part of Fannen's corps, the whole being commanded by lieutenant colonel Johnson.

General Wayne paid a visit to Stony Point about 12 o'clock at night;[3] and first from the picket a running fire was heard, which occasioned some alarm. A general silence followed for some time, during which the American officers held a council; and the English soldiers were dismissed to their tents.

But woe to the simple commander of Stony Point! When that undaunted hero general Wayne tickled their ears with "Remember the Paoli[4] and the massacre of Lady Washington's light horse at the Tappan." The grenadiers, in particular, of the 71st regiment, made for a while a gallant defense.

But neither the formidable rows of abatis nor the strong works in front and flank could damp the ardour of the American troops, who, in the face of an incessant and tremendous fire of musquetry, and cannon loaded with grape shot, broke their way through every obstacle until the van of each column met in the center of the fortress and obliged the surviving part of the garrison, amounting to upwards of 500 men, to surrender themselves prisoners at discretion.—

But let us pass over to our side of the river at Verplanck's— there you will not find a colonel Johnson, lying smug in his tent as at Stony Point; but you will find old colonel Webster, the Scotchman, ready cut and dry for you when the action commenced at the opposite fort. Four men out of each company turned out for a reserve guard, to receive the enemy when they should come across the river, as we expected nothing else but to be engaged front and rear at once; for we soon found Stony Point was taken, by their turning their artillery against us at Verplanck's, and commencing a dreadful cannonade, which necessarily obliged the shipping that lay in the river, to cut their cable and sail down.

But the Yankee army lay in our front eating molasses instead of attacking us.

Two or three days after this, the Americans commenced the evacuation of Stony Point, by destroying the works, dismounting the cannon, and removing their military stores and prisoners of war.

Among the number of vessels that came to carry off the booty was a row-galley laden with cannon and other stores, on our side of the river. Against this gallery we directed our artillery, and poured in a volley of grape and chain shot, which obliged the officers on board to desist from loading any further, and finding it impracticable to save the vessel, they spiked their cannon, and set fire to the galley which having burned to the water sunk with her cargo to the bottom.

The balance of the military stores were conveyed to West Point and the troops withdrawn. In ten days we also evacuated our fortress at Verplanck's and withdrew our troops to New York.

We lay that winter at a place called the Narrows on Long Island until Christmas Day, when an expedition was undertaken by Sir Henry Clinton and Admiral Abuthnot, against Charleston in South Carolina; as the conquest of the southern colonies was not meditated and considered as impracticable.

Our shipping lay on East River with the troops on board until the breaking of the ice, when several regiments were in the most imminent danger of being lost, particularly the 42nd, who were driven ashore with eight or ten ships, great and small. It was sometime in the spring before we could proceed in our voyage, being prevented by rough seas and tempestuous weather.

We set sail in very low spirits—our prospects were gloomy indeed—the very elements seemed to conspire against us, and threaten us with destruction. The distance between New York and Charleston is sailed in two weeks; but we were eight weeks on the passage.

The ship on which I was, being accidentally separated from the fleet in a storm, we were all in danger of being lost. The tempest blew with violence for about six hours.—We had 400 soldiers on board, and by the heaving and rolling of the ship, all the beds in which we lay broke loose from the sides of the vessel to which they were fastened, and the ship was so agitated by the wind and waves that she changed her position, so that our gunnels ran under water, and the guns on the same side broke loose on the quarterdeck.

The storm, however, having somewhat abated, we refreshed ourselves and cheered our hearts with a good can of grog, and pursued our voyage, hoping the worst was over and that we should soon get in sight of the fleet. But alas! all our pleasing expectations were frustrated; for after sailing a considerable time, we lost all hopes of ever coming up with the fleet.

A quarrel took place between some of the land and sea officers and a fight ensued in which the fire fell into the steerage and communicated into the hold, from which the smoke was immediately perceived to issue in curling volumes so that we expected every minute to be blown up. In this critical and perilous situation the cries of the women and children were truly distressing; and to render our danger still greater we were

again assailed with a violent squall; the waves rose like moun-
tains and threatened to overwhelm us; the ocean seemed to
open its bosom to receive us; the swelling surges broke in upon
us until we had five feet of water in the hold; our pumps were
choked, and for a while refused to perform their office. Our
condition was desperate.

But it pleased God to prolong our existence,—the fire was
extinguished; and by repeated attempts and strenuous exer-
tions we at length brought the pumps to work; the tempest
ceased and we continued on our voyage, still hoping to come up
with the fleet. Many a tedious hour did I sit on the foretop,
eagerly casting my eyes around to see if I could anywhere
descry a sail.

At length the wished for moment arrived; we espied our
fleet and soon joined it with joyful acclamations. The signal was
given for the different captains to go on board of the Convoy,
and a general invitation on board of the admiral's ship, where a
concert of music was held, and the soldiers and sailors got a
double allowance of rum to banish sorrow and exhilerate their
spirits.

We soon came in sight of land and took possession of St.
John Island near Charleston; 5,000 men were sent forward to
erect a right and left hand battery of 24 guns each. This was
accomplished the first night; and a centre battery the second
night.

An entrenchment was likewise dug in such a direction as to
have a communication from right to left; during which operation
we were played on by the batteries in the front of the town, by a
well-directed fire of grape, round and chain shot, with a great
number of bomb shells.—There was one line of batteries after
another until we came close to the canal; so that I have stood
many a time on one side of the canal, while the American
sentinel was directly opposite to me on the other side.

Though the offensive operations of the siege was conducted with great spirit and success, yet the town had still kept up a communication with the country on the farther side of Cooper River, and some bodies of militia, cavalry and infantry began to assemble on the higher part of that river, who, by keeping possession of the bridges might, at least, by cutting off supplies and molesting our foraging parties, have considerably retarded and disturbed the operation of our army.

To dislodge these troops, our general, as soon as his situation would permit, detached the 33d and 23d regiments and Tarleton's[5] light horse, in all about 1,400 men, under the command of lt. colonel Webster. We came on the enemy by surprise in the night, at Monk's corner,[6] and bloody work we had: being however victorious, we succeeded in our object of effectually stopping up the pass.

We remained at Monk's corner until the capitulation of general Lincoln,[7] after which we marched for Camden under the command of general Cornwallis and Lord Rawdon, with 1,500 effective infantry and 150 cavalry. When we arrived at Camden, a detachment was ordered to Ninety Six;[8] but it fell to my lot to continue at Camden, where I fell sick for the first and last time, that is, with common sickness; for I have been oftentimes indisposed with the bottle fever, and by wounds, bruises, and broken bones, and such like accidents.

While we continued at Camden we fared pretty well; only General (Horatio) Gates advanced to disturb our repose; and having encamped at a place called Ruggles, about 13 miles from Camden, he sent us word that "he would eat his dinner in Camden or in hell the next day." His forces were vastly superior to ours, at least in numbers, being computed at 5,000 to 6,000 men; the greater number of these consisted of militia, on whom little dependence could be placed.

Having received intelligence that general Gates had encamped in a bad situation, Lord Cornwallis mustered his troops and harangued them in words nearly to this effect:

"Now, my brave soldiers, now an opportunity is offered for displaying your valour, and sustaining the glory of British arms;—all you who are willing to face your enemies;—all you who are ambitious of military fame stand forward; for their are eight or ten to one coming against [us]; let the men who cannot bear the smell of gunpowder stand back and all you who are determined to conquer or die turn out."

Accordingly we all turned out except a few who were left to guard the sick and military stores. We marched out of Camden about 10 o'clock at night, August 15, 1780; it being the intention of our general to surprise the enemy in his quarters at Ruggles.

But in this we were disappointed, for Gen. Gates had set out about the same hour, in hopes to surprise us at Camden. We came up with their advanced party about seven miles from Camden, when the light troops and advanced guards on each side necessarily engaged each other in the dark. In this blind encounter, the American cavalry being driven back on the van, occasioned some disorder in their ranks; and having thus re-pelled them, we were eager for a general engagement; but Lord Cornwallis finding that the enemy were on bad ground, was unwilling to hazard in the dark the advantages which their situation would afford him in the light.

We then lay on our arms until daybreak, when both armies formed their lines, and approached within 100 yards of each other, and the Americans gave the first fire, which killed and wounded nearly one half of our number. We returned the fire and immediately charged on them with the bayonet. The action became general along the lines, and was supported with great obstinacy. The haziness of the morning prevented the ascent of the smoke, which occasioned such a thick cloud that it was difficult to observe the effects of a well supported fire on both sides.

It was discoverable, however, that the British troops were pushing forward and the Americans giving way; and after an obstinate resistance, for about three-quarters of an hour, the latter were thrown into confusion. We then opened to the right and left and let Tarleton's light horse pass through—Victory declared in our favor.

We took 900 prisoners and more are said to have been killed and wounded, but the precise number probably never ascertained. All their artillery amounting to 10 or 11 brass field pieces, with about 2,000 stands of arms, six stands of colours and all their baggage waggons, to the number of 150 fell into our hands.—The whole body of the militia (which constituted, as I have observed, the greater part of General Gates force) with the exception of only one North Carolina regiment, took to their heels the first fire, and though their general did all in his power to rally them, he could not persuade them to make a single stand, and so getting to the woods as fast as they could, they totally dispersed, leaving the continental regular troops to oppose the whole force of the British army.

It was a hard-fought battle, and the victory not very cheaply purchased on the side of the British; for even in one regiment (the 33d to which I belonged) not less than 116 out of 240 were killed and wounded. The whole loss may be estimated between 300 and 400 killed, wounded and missing; among these were several brave officers.

Lt. Col. Tarleton who had distinguished himself in this battle, was detached the next day with his cavalry, and the light infantry of the 23d regiment, called the English Fusiliers, in pursuit of General Sumter, who had retreated with a body of Americans and some cannon.

General Sumter, it seems, confiding in his distance from the enemy, was surprised in the middle of the day on the 18th of August, as his men were engaged in getting peaches in an orchard not far from the Catawba Fords.[9] Sumter himself having taken a number of tories, with a hogshead of rum and some provisions which they were carrying to the English army, was employed in dealing out the liquor, and was generous enough to give a gill to each prisoner, when Tarleton came upon him, killed 150 of his men and took 300 of them prisoners, with two pieces of cannon and several wagons.

The prisoners were conducted to Camden, and there treated with civility, and from thence they were sent off to Charleston under a guard of mounted infantry; but several of them were rescued by their countrymen before they could be carried to Charleston.

We lay in Camden until our wounded recovered, and then we marched on to Salisbury in North Carolina in close pursuit of the enemy, who had abandoned the town, leaving only a few sick tories in jail to die for want of water; and all the provisions they had were a few pounds of salt beef.—We were detained a few days in Salisbury in order to procure some provisions.

Had it not been for this delay, we might probably have overtaken general Morgan,[10] and retaliated upon him for Tarleton's defeat, and rescued the prisoners taken at the Cowpens.—This action in which the English were entirely routed, happened but a few weeks before; and for the bravery of the Americans and the address of their general merits a particular relation.

In order to prevent the Americans under general Morgan from taking possession of the valuable district of Ninety Six, Lord Cornwallis detached lt. col. Tarleton with 300 cavalry, 300 light infantry, the 7th regiment, the first battalion on the 71st regiment, and two 3-pounders. This force his Lordship thought sufficient to oppose the progress of Morgan; having full confidence in the success of Tarleton who had so highly distinguished himself in former engagements.

The British troops came up with the Americans on the 18th of January, 1781,[11] at a place called the Cowpens, near Pacolet river. General Morgan boldly stood on his defense, and drew up his troops with great judgment. The militia (composing about two-thirds of his force) were drawn up in a line on the edge of the wood, and exposed to open view; but the second line consisting of the continental and Virginia troops were out of sight in the wood itself, where they were drawn up in excellent order and ready for action.

The British, besides their field pieces, had the advantage of five to four in the infantry, and of more than three to one in cavalry. The attack was begun by the first line of infantry composed of the 7th regiment, and a body of light horse placed on each flank. The first battalion of the 71st regiment and the remainder of the light horse formed the reserve.

The American militia constituting the first line (as we said before) were unable to resist the assault (the Americans mistook a "wheel right" order for "retreat"), and immediately gave way; upon which the royal troops supposing the victory already gained, ardently pursued and were thereby thrown into some disorder.

Upon this, the second line of the Americans, having opened to the right and left to afford a passage to the fugitives, as well as to inclose their pursuers, as soon as they perceived the king's troops far enough advanced, poured in a close and deadly fire on both sides. The ground was instantly covered with the bodies of the killed and wounded, and a total rout ensued. Not less than 400 of the British infantry were either killed, wounded or taken prisoners.

The loss of the cavalry was not so much; but the colours of the 7th regiment, with the two field pieces fell into the hands of the Americans, and all the detachment of royal artillery were killed in defending their standard.

In this engagement, Colonel William Washington, who commanded a small detachment of American cavalry, had an opportunity of displaying his personal valour in a combat with colonel Tarleton, in which he cut off two of Tarleton's fingers and would have cut off his head had it not been for his stock buckle, which deadened the force of the stroke and saved the life of the British officer. They were both undoubtedly brave men, so that it remains a doubt with me to this day which of the two was a better soldier, when I consider that Washington was fighting for a good cause, and Tarleton for a bad one.

However, be that as it may, colonel Washington, I believe, to this day (if he be alive) carries a mark on two of his fingers, which he received in his encounter with colonel Tarleton.

But on this occasion, colonel Tarleton was glad to make his escape with the small remainder of his army. This defeat was very mortifying to Lord Cornwallis; and I myself was an eyewitness when at the first interview between him and Tarleton, the account of the disaster brought tears from Cornwallis's eyes; lamenting, no doubt, the loss of so many brave soldiers.

The Cowpens prisoners were pushed off toward Winchester in Virginia, and we pursued in hopes of overtaking Morgan before he crossed the Yadkin river, a few miles from Salisbury; but in this we were deceived, as we had been before in several of our bad undertakings.

We then returned back some distance and took a route by the Morgvian towns, and encamped one night on a rising ground contiguous to one of these towns, the inhabitants of which were very generous in rolling out their whiskey barrels to make us drunk.

The Moravians were always suspected of being tories, but on this occasion, we had reason to think differently, by their liberality in furnishing us so abundantly with spiritous liquors, as all the world knows that a soldier's chief delight is in drinking. And, I believe, had the Americans been vigilant, they would have succeeded in their insidious design, for it is my candid opinion that there were not fifty sober men among us, for it was a very rainy night and we had suffered for want of drink, as well as through fatigue.

But we fortunately escaped being discovered, and lay

there secure for some time.—We next directed our march toward Charlotte, and coming within two miles of the town, the enemy formed a line of battle; but we advanced on them and they retreated; and a running fight ensued, until we came to the town, where they made a stand for a while, but we rushed on them with the bayonet, and they again retreated. We pursued them for about 7 miles; but they were too swift on foot for us; so finding that we could not come up with them, we returned back to Charlotte.

The next day a guard was sent to Rigley's Mills in order to do duty there and I turned baker for the guard (and a little for myself).

We continued there for some time—but now comes the trouble—the enemy got a reenforcement of 3,000 or 4,000 men and we had to run back faster than we came. We made our retreat like lost sheep, not knowing where to go, no forage, no provisions for our men, though marching day and night. At this time I saw an English guinea offered for a bit of cornbread not larger than my two fingers.—Hard times with us indeed—16 days without a morsel of bread.

In this starving condition we made our retreat to Wynnesborough, [Winnsboro] 40 miles from Camden, where we fixed our winter quarters and sent to Camden for provisions which soon were brought us by water, and then we fared sumptuously; being plentifully supplied with all sorts of provisions, and having our back rations paid up.

In relating the various incidents of my life, I should deem myself guilty of an unpardonable omission, were I to pass on without mentioning the circumstances of a fist fight, which I had when we were quartered in Wynnesborough and the first that I ever had since I came to the years of discretion.

There was a certain Bill Airton, a butcher, who was a mess mate of mine, and had often endeavored to provoke me to a fight; but as I always considered him a stouter man than myself, and being besides unacquainted with the art of boxing (as it is called) I had constantly declined his invitations, and endeavored to keep clear of all private quarrels.

It happened, however, one day, when myself and several of my companions made a fire before our wigwam, that Mr. Airton, who had been absent while the fuel was gathering, came up to the fire, and in a very abrupt manner says to me, "Shaw, d---n you stand back, you have no right here, d---n you, stand back." Giving me at the same time such a blow to the eye as made my head sing psalms for some time.

The sergeant then coming up, and, understanding the circumstances, says, "Shaw, you must fight and whip him or else I will whip you." So we buckled to it in our buff; and having a good second helped the cause very much on my side; for a good officer makes a good soldier. Inspired with confidence through the encouragement of the sergeant, I soon gave Mr. Airton an Irishman's coat of arms, i. e., two black eyes and a bloody nose, which made him a good friend ever after.

> "Poor John and the butcher then stript to their buffs,
> Fell to work and engaged in what's called fisticuffs;
> And so the big butcher that would be a brawling
> And picking a quarrel, at last got a mauling."

Chapter 3

"To show I don't flinch fill the
bowl up again
Then give me a pinch of your
sneezing, a yean.

—Dean Swift

It was early in the spring (1781) before we set out; and then we took our route to Hillsborough [Hillsboro] where we set up the royal standard; and our general by a proclamation invited all loyal subjects to repair to it and assist in restoring order and government. But though we had been led to believe that the king had many friends in that part of the country, yet the event did not answer our expectations. The royalists were but few, and most of them too timid to join the king's standard. A part of them, indeed, under the command of a certain colonel Pyle, had set out with a view of joining us at Hillsborough; but they were accidentally met by a detachment of the American army and most of them cut off.

We staid at Hillsborough about a week and all got completely shod.—We left town in the night and made a movement toward the Haw River, marching by the way of the Rocky Ford.

We came up with the enemy by the river side, and having formed a line, we exchanged a few shots, and then advanced to give them the bayonet; but they retreated and crossed the river,

and then we had a standing fight; and though we had orders not
to cross the river, yet the front line consisting of the 33d, 23d
and 71st regiments, the Irish volunteers, and the Yagers, under
Lord Rawdon, would not be stopped by anything.

So we crossed the Rocky Ford, and hot works we had; but
we beat them off and formed a line on the same side of the river
which they had occupied and soon put them to flight and
pursued them for 14 miles, until we lost sight of them.

We then directed our march toward Guilford Courthouse
and halted about three or four miles from town. At this time the
scarcity of provisions was so great that we had but one pound of
flour for six men per day with very little beef and no salt the half
of the time.

With this allowance, my mess mates and I made two meals
a day, which we managed by first boiling the beef, and then
taking it out and having mixed our pound of flour with some
water we put it into the kettle in which the beef had been
boiled; and when sufficiently heated, we took it off the fire and
let it stand until it cooled. This served us for breakfast and the
beef we kept for dinner; and as for supper we were obliged to do
without it.

On one occasion, the officers, having by some means
neglected to put out sentinels on guard for three hours together,
impelled by hunger we took the blessed opportunity of going
out in search of something to satisfy our craving appetite.

A soldier of the 23d by the name of Tattesdell and myself
made a push for the country.—We had not gone above a mile
until we came to a house in hopes to get something to eat; but
the house was already full of soldiers upon the same business;
and I heard the woman of the house crying, "I will go and tell
your officers."

Upon hearing these words, my comrade and I proceeded
forward about three or four miles, until we came to a fine, open
plantation, and an elegant framed house belonging to a major

Bell of the American army. So we entered the house, where we found an old lady and her two daughters—we saluted them with as much politeness as our awkward manners would admit of; and the old lady very civily asked us to sit down.

We soon told her our business, that we wanted some flour; upon which she immediately filled our knapsacks; and invited us to stay until something could be made ready, which invitation we readily accepted; and I very well remember that I got some of the best Johnny-cake I ever ate in my life.

While we were partaking of the delicious repast, for to us it was truly delicious, a conversation arose.

Says the old lady, "Now if you will go with what you have gotten, and join our boys, I will give you my two daughters, and a complete suit of clothes apiece."

"But," we argued, "the bad consequences of desertion, that it was death by the law, and that even if we could bring ourselves to act so dishonourable a part as to desert our colours, yet death by shooting or hanging was a thing not much to be desired."

But by the bye, I must inform the reader that for my part, if I could have entertained the smallest hopes of succeeding in gaining the affections of either of the young ladies, so lovely were they in my eyes, I would cheerfully have hazarded my life and taken the old lady at her word; for I thought them the most beautiful creatures my eyes ever beheld.

But as such good fortune was not to be expected, and we had no time to delay, my comrade and I, after we had finished our meal, took our leave of the old lady, thanking her for her charity, and immediately departed.

Scarcely had we gone half way up the lane when seven of Lee's[1] light horse made their appearance; my companion swore there was Tarleton's light horse coming, and, says he, "we shall be taken up on suspicion of plundering and get 500 lashes apiece."

"No," said I, upon observing their brown coats and white cockades, "no, my friend, you are deceived; these must be the rebels."

Having therefore discovered his mistake, he began to cry;—but for my part, I thought it very good fortune. As they were advancing toward us, we concluded to go and meet them; which we did, and falling on our knees, begged for quarter, which they granted us and said, "Come on, we will give you good quarters."

And so on we went past the house that had betrayed us—it was fine fun for the old lady to see how handsomely she had tricked us.

They brought us on a short distance beyond major Bell's, and there were Washington and Lee light horse and Morgan's riflemen. These officers examined us as to the strength of Cornwallis's army and sent us under general guard to general Greene's encampment,[2] and while the guard were conducting us thither, they suffered one of Morgan's subaltern officers to strip us; against which conduct we remonstrated, my observing that no British officer would permit a continental soldier to be stripped while a prisoner of war.

But we were obliged to submit, for the officer drew his sword and swore if we did not comply he would run us through. So they took our clothes, not leaving us even our leggings or shoes; and God knows, they wanted them badly; for such ragged mortals I never saw in my life before, to pass under the character of soldiers.

We were then brought to the camp on the 11th day of March, 1781, and after being reexamined by General Greene, we were sent to the provost, where we found about 30 fellow prisoners who had been taken on straggling parties. From thence we were sent to Halifax courthouse, where we remained until after the battle of Guilford, which took place the 15th of

March, [1781] and was one of the hardest fought battles that
ever happened in America.

And as a brief description of this memorable battle may not
be perhaps unacceptable to some of my young readers, I shall
present them with an abstract of the most remarkable facts and
circumstances from the best information I could obtain, and
with as much impartiality as possible.

On the morning of the 15th of March, Lord Cornwallis with
all his forces, consisting of 5,000 or 6,000 men, with a view
either to meet the Americans under general Greene, or to attack
them in their encampment. A few miles from Guilford the
advanced guard under colonel Tarleton fell in with colonel
Lee's legion and some militia and was, at last, obliged to retreat.

The American army under general Greene was about equal
to the British in number and posted on a rising ground, about a
mile and a half from Guilford courthouse. The Americans were
drawn up in three lines; the front line was composed of two
brigades of North Carolina militia under the generals Richard
Butler and Eaton; the second line consisting of two brigades of
Virginia militia commanded by the generals Stephens and Law-
son; and the third line, also of two brigades of continental or
regular troops commanded by general Isaac Hugar & colonel
Otho Williams.

Colonel Washington, with the dragoons of the first and
third regiments, a detachment of continental light infantry, and
a regiment of riflemen under colonel Lynch, formed a separate
body to cover the right flank; while colonel Lee with the legion,
a detachment of light infantry, and colonel William Campbell's
riflemen, formed a corps of observation for the security of the
left flank.

The British commander disposed his troops in the following order: On the right, the Hessian regiment of Von Bose, with
the 71st regiment led on by general Alexander Leslie, and

supported by the first battalion of guards. On the left were the
23d and 33d regiments, led on by Colonel Webster, supported
by the grenadiers and the 2nd battalion of guards commanded
by general O'Hara. The Germans and the light infantry of the
guards remained in the woods on the left of the guns, and the
cavalry under colonel Tarleton was drawn up in the road, ready
to act as circumstances might require.

The action commenced by a dreadful cannonade about
one o'clock in the afternoon. The discharge of the artillery
(which lasted about 20 minutes) having ceased the British
troops advanced in three columns, and attacked the Carolina
militia with great fury, and soon forced them to quit the field.
But the Virginia militia gave them a warm reception, and kept
up a heavy fire for a considerable time, till they also were beaten
back, and the action became general almost everywhere.

The thickness of the wood rendered the British bayonets
of little service, until the second battalion of the guards gained
the clear ground near Guilford courthouse, and having drawn
up in an open field on the left side of the road, attacked them
with vigor and defeated them, taking two six-pounders; but as
they pursued the Americans into the woods, they were thrown,
in their turn, into great confusion by a heavy and well directed
fire from the Americans, and furiously charged and driven back
by Colonel Washington's dragoons, with the loss of the two six-
pounders they had taken.

But the American cavalry were again repulsed, and the two
six-pounders fell once more into the hands of the British. The
victory for a while seemed doubtful, but after several bloody
conflicts, in which great bravery was displayed on both sides,
the American general thought it prudent to order a retreat.

Many of the militia dispersed through the woods; but the
continental troops made a very orderly retreat.

The British general remained master of the field, and
consequently claimed the victory.—But it was a dear bought

victory; for the loss on the side of the British, according to the account of Lord Cornwallis himself, was 532 killed, wounded and missing. Several of their bravest officers fell in the action, and amongst the rest, my good old colonel Webster received a mortal wound—he was as gallant an officer as ever drew the sword—I served in his regiment five years and some months.[3]

General Greene, in the account he sent to congress stated the loss of the continental forces at 329 killed, wounded and missing; in which number, however, the loss of the militia was not included; it amounts to upwards of 100.

In this battle a few prisoners were taken by the Americans, and sent forward to join us at Halifax courthouse; and in a short time we were marched on to Winchester in Virginia, where we joined the Cowpens prisoners, and were put into barracks a few miles from the town, under a strong guard.

Here we suffered much: our houses had no covering to shelter us from the inclemency of the weather; and we were exposed to cold, hunger and want of clothing; and all manner of ill treatment, insult and abuse.

Having thus, for a considerable time (I cannot say with the patience of Job) endured many hardships, we formed a project for our escape, by means of one of the guard, who agreed for three half joes[4] to conduct us to New York. The time and mode of elopement being fixed upon, we parted with our uniforms and put ourselves in disguise ready for the journey.

But when the appointed hour arrived, we found ourselves deceived by the fellow's wilful neglect in fulfilling his promise, but what better could we expect from a tory and traitor;—He that would turn tory is worse than a devil; for, be the devil as bad as he may be is still said to be true to his party.

So we had to continue in our confinement as refugees. But some time in the summer, we were ordered to be ready to march at a moment's warning; and soon after a new guard was appointed to conduct us to Lancaster in Pennsylvania.

The cruelty of this new guard exceeded anything we had yet seen; their conduct was indeed shameful and altogether incompatible with the profession of either soldiers or christians; they drove us like so many bullocks to the slaughter.

Scarcely had we advanced three miles before the captain broke his broad sword by cutting and slashing the prisoners, who were too much weakened by hunger and former ill treatment to keep up in the march. The lieutenant, a snotty-nosed stripling, just from the chimney corner, came up, raging like a madman, with his small sword in his hand, and pushed it with such violence into the back of one of my fellow prisoners, that he broke it in the wound, where it remained until one of his comrades pulled it out.

Now such dastardly conduct towards poor prisoners of war, who had no weapon to defend themselves, was a disgrace, even to chimney-corner officers. However, we marched along as well as we could, consoling ourselves with the hopes of being delivered one day or other from such cruel bondage.

We came to a place where there was a mill turned by a stream, the source of which was not more than 100 yards above the mill;—here we expected to draw some provisions, but were sadly disappointed, as we had been three days without any, and through perfect weakness, I trembled like a patient in a severe fit of the ague. All we drew was but one ear of corn per man, and this was a sweet morsel to us; we softened it in water, and grated it on the lid of our camp kettle and made bread of it.

This we did until we came to Fredericktown barracks, where we drew provisions, and found the people more hospitable and kind; many of them having experienced the hardships and calamities of war; and at the same time they had several of their friends and relatives, then prisoners with the English, and suffering much greater hardships than I ever experienced while a prisoner with the Americans.

But it is natural for every man to think his own case the

hardest; and though of ill usage I had my share, yet I enjoyed the fresh air, while thousands of soldiers lay languishing and dying in loathsome prison ships, stinking jails, and dark dungeons, deprived of the privilege of the fresh air, necessary to preserve health; and even excluded from the cheerful light of heaven, and having nothing for subsistence but damaged provisions, such as even a wretch starving on the gibbet and ready to eat the flesh off his own body with hunger, might turn from with disgust.

Such was the unhappy situation of those who were taken at Long Island, Fort Washington, Brandywine, Germantown, Monmouth, Camden and several other places. Indeed the treatment of the prisoners in general during the American war was harsh, severe, and in many instances, inhuman; except only with regard to those who were taken under a capitulation; for such were always treated well.

Burgoyne's and Cornwallis's men were treated like gentlemen, to my own certain knowledge, and why not the soldier who is taken prisoner in the field of action, or in any other way discharging his duty to his king or country?

We next arrived at Lancaster, where we had reason to expect good treatment, the inhabitants being in general remarkable for hospitality, and for contributing to the relief of objects of distress.—While in Lancaster I became acquainted with a man in the army, belonging to the 44th regiment, whom I think proper to mention in this place on account of his piety.

I had frequently observed him retiring into a secret place, which at length awakened my curiosity to see what he was about;—I watched him, and found he went there to pray; he was remarkably reserved in all his conduct and conversation; was often alone, and seldom spoke, except when spoken to; and from his general deportment, I firmly believe he was what is truly a phenomenon in the army, a conscientious christian.

But this pious example had little influence on my conduct.

One day, I very well remember, I got a quarter of a dollar from a Mr. John Hoover, by dint of hard begging; I now fancied myself as rich as a king, and immediately sent for a loaf of bread and a pint of whiskey, with which I and my comrades regaled ourselves, and sung some merry songs, being for the time as happy as princes.

Not long after, before we left Lancaster, we concerted another scheme for our release, by undermining, from one of the cellars under the barrack yard and stockades, about 100 yards, and coming out in the graveyard—conveying the dirt in our pockets, and depositing it in the necessary house and other private places.

The next thing was to seize the magazine which contained a large quantity of ammunition and firelocks, with which we intended to arm ourselves, and being joined by a strong party of tories, set fire to the town, and so proceed to form a junction with the English army.

But our evil designs were entirely frustrated, by one of our own men belonging to the 71st regiment, of the name of Burk, who first made our plot known to the officer of the guard; and being conducted to General Wayne, who was then in Lancaster, gave in all the names of the non-commissioned officers.

The consequence of this was that about 11 o'clock at night, General Wayne came to the barracks with a guard of militia, and called out those unhappy men, and marched them down to the jail and put them in close confinement. And the commissary of prisoners, whose name was Hobley, ordered a ditch to be dug at the foot of the stockades, 7 or 8 feet deep, and filled with large stones, to prevent us from undermining; and had pieces of scantling spiked along the top and bottom of the stockades.

The prisoners were employed to do the work, and they very cunningly cut the spikes in two, so as to go through the scantling and but slightly penetrate the stockades. These short spikes were put in at the bottom in order that the stockade might swing when cut off underground.

A day or two after this when Mr. Hobley the commisary of prisoners came to call the roll, a man of Lord Rawdon's corps, whose name has slipped my memory, took the commissary aside, and offered to shew him all the private ways by which the prisoners went out and in. Accordingly he went around the stockades with the commissary, and made all the discovery he could.

When all was done, and the fellow wanted to be discharged, Mr. Hobley called the prisoners together and represented to them the bad policy of one prisoner turning traitor against the rest, and concluded with telling the fellow he ought to be hanged for acting so much like a scoundrel.

We accordingly held a court martial, and the fellow pleaded guilty, and was sentenced to receive 500 lashes on his bare posteriors, well laid on with a broad leathern strap.

Soon after this, two of my fellow prisoners and myself laid a plan for our escape, which we effected in the following manner:—the night being appointed for the purpose, we procured a large knife, with which about 2 o'clock in the morning we had dug about two feet underground, where, to our great joy, we found the stockade rotten, or at least considerably decayed.

We cut away by turns until the stockade swung by the upper spike; so the boldest fellow went foremost, and the sentry fired at the hindmost; but we all escaped to a rye field where we lay hidden for a while, and then made the best of our way to a friend's house, two miles from town, and found there 30 or 40 more lying in a barn.

Next morning, each man taking his own road, I directed my course for the Moravian town[5] (as it is called) 8 miles from Lancaster, and there I met with a friendly reception from a certain Joseph Willey, one of the Moravian society, a wool weaver by occupation, and a native of the town of Putsey in Yorkshire, old England.

This man, though a friend to individuals, particularly those from Yorkshire, was notwithstanding a true republican in principle, and as warm an advocate for the rights and liberties of America as any man could be.

He recommended me to the brethren of his society as a prisoner of war belonging to a christian nation, and an object of compassion, and prayed for their assistance; which they granted and furnished me with what I stood in need of; but not until they had exacted a promise from me that I would return to my captivity, and wait with patience for the exchange of prisoners.

This promise I fulfilled, and accordingly returned to Lancaster barracks. And in a few days after my return, an officer of an additional company of the 33d regiment taken with general Burgoyne's troops, came to Lancaster, and an application was made for some money, and each man received five guineas; there were 16 of us in a room together making ourselves as happy as possible, and we were determined to have a general feast or frolic.

Accordingly having laid in provisions of different sorts and procured a barrel of whiskey in the morning, I leave you to guess, my courteous reader, what an appearance we made by the middle of the day, when a pot-pie was proposed for dinner, and the preparation of it undertaken by a drunken old soldier who, in making up the crust of the pie, used whiskey instead of water; the dough being made and rolled out, and put in the pot.

The ingredients of the pie were added consisting of old rancid bacon, dried apples and onions and old chews of tobacco; and when sufficiently baked at the fire, the whole compound was next stewed in good old whiskey. And when ready a general invitation was given to the neighbors to partake of this "delicate" repast.

And we concluded the entertainment with a good bucket

of whiskey, dancing with our shirts off while we were able to stand, and then we lay down promiscuously, and slept til morning.

Our frolic resembled so much the Irish feast, as described by Dean Swift, that I cannot forbear transcribing a few lines from the poet:

> "We danced in a round, Cutting capers and romping;
> A mercy the ground Did not burst with our stamping.
> The floor was all wet With leaps and with jumps,
> While the water and sweat Splish splash in our pumps.
> Bless you late and early Laughlin O'Enagin
> By my hand, you dance rarely, Margery Grinagin.
> Bring straw for my bed Shake it down to the feet,
> Then over us spread The winnowing sheet.
> To show I don't flinch Fill the bowl up again,
> Then give us a pinch Of your sneezing, a yean."

Next morning myself and a certain McGowan, after taking a little more of the usquebaugh, determined to try our fortune; and accordingly made application for a pass for a few hours, and a sentry to go as a safeguard to bring us back at the expiration of the limited time.

Previously to this, we had made ourselves acquainted with a certain militiaman by the name of Everman, a tobacco spinner, who lived in Lancaster, and a notorious drunkard. We called on him, and he readily attended us to a certain Tom Mahoney's, who kept the Sign of the White Horse in Donnegal Street, near the barracks.

So now, Mr. Everman, "What will you please to drink?"

"What you please, gentlemen," said Mr. Everman.

So a lusty bowl of punch was called for, and we all drank heartily together, until our sentry got drunk, and fell asleep on his guard.

We seized the favorable opportunity, and set out to push our fortune; and in order to avoid suspicion, we soon parted and took different roads. I came to a farmer's house and inquired for work. The farmer very readily agreed to give me employment.

"But what," says he, "can you do?"

I told him I was brought up a stuff weaver.

"Can you weave worsted?" says he.

"Yes, sir," said I.

"Well, then," said he, "if you will weave a piece of worsted I have on hands, and continue with me five weeks, I will teach you to be a linen weaver."

I consented and fulfilled the contract, and he made me an indifferent linen weaver.

After that I parted with my new master and went to live with one John Bostler, a Dutchman. The family consisted of the old man and his wife and three daughters.—I was very much at a loss to understand their language, as none of them could speak English but the old man, who spoke it in a very broken manner.

This circumstance was to me an insurmountable obstacle, as it prevented all conversation with the female part of the family; and to be candid, I should have had no objection to pay court to one of this Dutchman's daughters; for they were fine, hearty, industrious girls. But finding it impractical I left Mr. Bostler and set out with a view of going to Coleman's furnace.[6]

But before I got there I fell in with one William Cassel, who had a large store building on hand, at the Cross-roads,[7] leading to Lancaster, Stickle's tavern, Grubb forge and Hornet's tavern.

Here was the second well I ever dug. It was 65 feet deep, and in digging we came to a cavern in the side of the wall in which we could have turned a wagon and team, and at the depth of 26 feet, with some other curiosities too tedious to mention here.

After completion of this well I went to work for Christo-

pher Laby, a moneist by profession; and here was the first
quarry I ever wrought in. After I had been at the quarrying
business for some time, I had the misfortune to break three of
my ribs.

To the Cross-roads there was a resort of all descriptions of
men, from furnaces and forges; prisoners of war and deserters
from both the English and continental army; and men of diabolical principles and practices from almost all quarters employed
in card playing, cock fighting, horse racing, billiard playing,
long-bullet playing, fiddling and dancing, drinking and carous-
ing, no matter what day of the week, though the Sabbath was
the more frequently chosen for such practices.

A party of us had agreed to go one Sunday morning to
Captain Huston's (commonly called Hornet's) tavern, in order
to drink bitters and to take a game at long bullets close by the
Dutch meetinghouse. And while the good people were at
sermon and praying to the Great Author of all things to turn our
hearts away from evil ways, I was chose to look out for the
bullets, and on a sudden one of the bullets struck me on the
head, and knocked me down, where I lay, to the great con-
sternation of all, for some time before the company could tell
what was best to be done with me.

But at length some signs of life appearing, they removed
me to the tavern in a very dangerous situation; for by this
unlucky accident a fracture was made in my skull which so
disturbed my brain that ever after, if I drank spiritous liquors, a
temporary frenzy was produced which caused me to conduct in
a most extravagant and outrageous manner.

I was not the only person that received punishment for his
immoral and irregular practices; for many of my acquaintances
fell victim to the same, and among the rest were Curtis Grubb
and Peter Grubb; the former of whom in one of his frolics
jumped into the furnace in full blast; and the latter by putting a
pistol into his mouth blew out his brains. These with several

other instances of the ruinous effects of dissipation and of keeping bad company were, and perhaps justly, considered by the good people of the vicinity as a judgment from heaven upon those wretches for their impiety.

As soon as I was able to work, I finished the job I had undertaken, and went to live with a certain Hugh H-gg-y, a few miles from Lancaster, with whom I took up my winter quarters. Mr. H-- -- was very much addicted to getting drunk and lying out in the woods, which made his wife very uneasy; but as good luck would have it, he had a dog that always accompanied his master, and when any misfortune befell him, the dog would come running home and alarm the family.

Upon which occasion I had to set out in search of him, through the thickest woods, and frequently when it was so dark that I could not see my hand before me; my dependence being entirely on the dog. But he never failed to lead me to the place where his master lay.

During my stay here I fared pretty well, and lived with some degree of contentment until a circumstance occurred, which obliged me to leave the house. Mr. H. one night at home got very groggy, was in a very ill humor, and swore "he would have revenge that night" and accordingly he ordered his wife to bring him some more grog, which she did, and handed him the bottle and some water.

Having drunk what suited him, he began to curse and swear at his wife, calling her a d---d strumpet, and loading her with every opprobrius epithet which his indignation suggested.

She endeavored by mild words to pacify him and bring him to reason, but this only made him more furious.—He knocked her down, and jumped with his knees on her breast, and then pulling out his knife, swore he would kill her on the spot.

Now I thought it would be wrong in me to stand by and see murder committed without endeavoring to prevent it; so I took him by the collar and pulled him off until she made her escape.

This interference of mine, which I thought perfectly justifiable, was likely to produce such domestic broils that for the peace of the poor woman I thought it most prudent to leave the house; which I did and went to live with one Captain Wilhelm, an inn-keeper who lived about three miles from Lancaster.

I happened to be in one of my mad frolics one day when three continental officers came on a visit to captain Wilhelm's.—I was pretty tipsy and caused the officers to inquire, who was I?

They were told I was a prisoner of war and by name John R. Shaw.

Being afraid therefore that such inquiries might lead to a detection, and that some person for a reward might deliver me up to the British who, at that time, offered a half joe for every British prisoner brought to them at Lancaster, I was brought to a stand what to do in this delicate circumstance.

Upon a little reflection, however, I was determined against having any further connection with the English army; but if I could by any artiface get enlisted in the American army, as the war was, in all probability, nearly at an end, I should soon get my liberty, and be released from the hardships of military duty, of which I was pretty well tired.

But there was an act of congress against the enlisting of prisoners of war, which made my undertaking rather desperate; however, as I knew that many others in the same condition had got admittance, and that there were several hundreds of prisoners, who now enlisted in the different corps of the American army, I resolved to try my fortune by inventing the most plausible fiction which I could devise in order to prevent suspicion and detection.

So on I went to Lancaster, where I soon met with the recruiting sergeant whose name was Townsel, an old British deserter. But according to the good old adage, always set a rogue to catch a rogue,—I sauntered about a little while before he

took notice of me; but at length he asked me if I would enlist for
a soldier.

I pretended to be very much alarmed, and told him I was
not acquainted with the life of a soldier, and was afraid to go to
war.

"Well, but," says the sergeant, "you are a prisoner of war,
are you not?"

"No sir," said I. "I never was a soldier in my life."

"Where did you come from?"

"I came from Little Chickes,[8] and served my time with
one William Curran."

"How long did you serve?"

"I served four years and I can prove it by my indentures,
and by a number of respectable gentlemen in the neighborhood, such as Alexander Scott, and captain Scott, with many
others."

"Well, Shaw," said the sergeant, "you have a fine story
truly, and I hope you will stick to it; for you must know that a liar
has need of a good memory. So look sharp or else you will be
caught. Well, Mr. Shaw, we must go to the officers."

So we went to the captains Doil and Powers.

"Well, gentlemen," says the sergeant, "here is another
recruit for you."

"Young man, where did you come from?"

"I came from Little Chickes."

"With whom did you live there?"

"My last residence was at Coleman's furnace."

"And what did you follow?"

"I followed working at the mine banks."

"But with whom did you live at Little Chickes?"

"I served my time with Mr. Curran, and I can prove it by
my indentures and by men of the first respectability, such as
Alexander Scott and his nephew captain Scott."

So without asking me any further questions, they gave me

three half joes as bounty money, and I went with the recruiting
sergeant to quarters, where my new companions used all the
means in their power to jockey me out of my money, but "it is
not easy to catch old birds with chaff." I was not so raw a soldier
as they ignorantly supposed nor so easily imposed on as they
imagined; for I deposited my money with the officer, and drew
it as I stood in need.

But by this conduct I got a good deal of ill will among those
sharpers.

But by this time Cornwallis was taken and the weary
regiment to which I belonged while in the British service had
come to Lancaster; and in a few days I was attacked by the
sergeant major, who called me a d---n rebel. And upon returning to the rendezvous, I made my complaint to the lieutenant,
who had been an old British deserter, and from whom I had
received singular favors.

I was now made a corporal and a cutlass was given me to
enable me to stand in my own defense against the British
officers, who often threatened to take me out of the ranks. But
they soon ceased to disturb me, for there were but few in our
recruiting party who were not prisoners of war.

Having been with the recruiting party for some time, I got
acquainted with some of the congress regiment soldiers to my
cost; for as I was walking the streets of Lancaster with one of
them, he robbed me of my handkerchief and money, in open
daylight. This may be called complete street robbery.

We stayed there until we enlisted nearly 300 men, and
most of them prisoners of war; and then we were sent to Carlisle
barracks,[9] by which time the Pennsylvania line was broken, and
formed into three regiments (i. e. the 1st, 2nd, and 3d). It was
my lot to belong to the 3d regiment, commanded by that
undaunted hero, colonel Richard Butler (who afterward fell in
St. Clair's defeat)[10] and the honourable George Bush's company: (the son of Squire Bush of Wilmington).

We lay here a considerable time, and I began to grow weary
of the single life, and paid my addresses to a certain young
woman, who was at service in the family of a Mr. Samuel Stuart,
inn-keeper in York Street, Carlisle; and after a short courtship
we were married at the home of Mr. Robert Johnston, a respectable citizen, who gave us a good dinner, and in the evening, I
was conducted to the barracks, with my new bride, by a number
of soldiers of the first respectability.

> "Imprimis, at the temple porch Stood Hymen with a flaming
> torch;
> The smiling Cyprian Goddess brings Her infant loves with
> purple wings;
> And pigeons billing, sparrows treading, Fair emblem of a
> faithful wedding;
> Behold the bridegroom and his bride, Walk hand in hand and
> side by side;
> She by the tender graces drest, But he by Mars, in martial
> vest. —
> And then to make the matter sure, Dame Juno brought a priest
> demure.
> Luna was absent on pretense Her time was not till nine
> months hence.
> The rites performed, the parson paid, In state returned the
> grand parade; —
> But still the hardest part remains."
> But—" I pity the ladies so modest and nice."

The young woman whom I married was a native of Ireland,
and from the town of Sligo, and by profession a Roman Cath-
olic; her maiden name was Mary O'Hara, who, before the
commencement of the American Revolution, came in a re-
demptioner, and served out her time in Kishicocles [Kishaco-

quillas] valley, in the family of a certain Robert Homes, and always supported a good character.

I did everything in my power to render my connubial life as comfortable as the nature of our circumstances would permit. I endeavoured to gain the goodwill of the officers, and got permission to work in the town, and by the recommendation and interest of one Robert Gibson, I met with employment from Mr. John Creech, a merchant in whose services I continued while the army lay at Carlisle.

Chapter 4

"I would not kiss the maid when I could kiss the mistress; but both rather than be called nice."

Some time in the summer of 1782 we were ordered on an Indian expedition to a place called the Standing Stone.[1] We marched by way of Callender's Mills, and so on to Sherman valley, to Juniata, and then to Kishicocles valley, by way of Squire Brown's where we lay for a short time; and some of our men got to plundering, and being caught in the act, were tried and sentenced to receive 100 lashes apiece, which they got well laid on.

Our expedition, however, was rendered unnecessary, as the Indians were dispersed without our assistance. We then returned to Carlisle, soon after which the great anniversary of American independence was celebrated;[2] and on this occasion a well conducted representation of a battle was exhibited by the 3d Pennsylvania regiment, and the town militia consisting of one company of foot, and one of horse, with a small redoubt erected in front of the town, commanded by colonel Richard Butler, whose name ought never to be forgotten.

The day was spent to the great satisfaction of all spectators, and the scene closed with an elegant ball, honoured with the attendance of nearly 100 ladies of the first character, both in town and country.

Soon after this an affair of a more unpleasant nature happened:—a certain sergeant Thompson, who was on guard over a few prisoners who were confined for desertion, being provoked by the ill language of one of them, seized a firelock and with it beat out the poor prisoner's brains.

The sergeant indeed in his defense alleged that Robertson arose from the guard bed with an intent to force the sentry. However, the murderer was immediately arrested and sent to jail under a strong guard, and confined in irons, where he lay until his trial came on. But one thing was much in his favor, he had always supported a good character, and was generally esteemed in the army.

He was tried and tried again; for colonel Butler was determined to save him, guilty or not guilty.[3] Horrid indeed were the cries and screams of the murderer while in the dungeon:—he was constantly exclaiming in the most frantic manner, "Here he comes in a flame of fire! He will catch me! O here he stands! He stands here grinning at me! O, guilty, guilty conscience—how I am tormented!"

If the torment of a guilty conscience be so great in this world, what must it be in the next!—This wretch escaped hanging, but he died a miserable death not long after.

At the same time two deserters were tried, and condemned to be hanged; and when the day came for their execution, they were brought to the gallows, and a circle formed, a hangman was wanted, as there was a number of other prisoners brought out who had been condemned for different crimes.

Accordingly lieutenant Butler, who did the duty of an adjutant, made choice of an old man by the name of O'Connor to be hangman; but the old man positively refused to perform the office, and said he would die rather than accept it. He was then tied up to the foot of the gallows for his disobedience and received 100 lashes well laid on, which he bore without a murmur, and was then ordered into the ranks.

A man by the name of Burns was next pitched upon to perform the honourable office, and after some hesitation he complied, and put the rope on the neck of one of the criminals; but before any of them were swung off, a reprieve came, to the joy of all the spectators, and all were dismissed. The intended hangman was knocked and kicked about like a dog, while Mr. O'Connor was applauded by every soldier in the garrison, and treated with all imaginable respect for his manly conduct.

In a few days after that, a small party of us was ordered to McCollister's town in pursuit of deserters.[4] The party consisted of sergeant McGilton, corporal Webb, a man by the name of McCollister (as great a scoundrel as ever came from Ireland) and one Myres, and myself; being only five in number.

We pursued our journey until we came to Yellow Breeches Creek, and so on to Conewago,[5] where we stopped to take some refreshment; and some country people coming in, we asked them to drink with us, which they readily did, and having spent some time in conversation with them, the sergeant asked one of them if he would enlist; but as he seemed not very willing, the conversation was dropped and we proceeded on our way, all but McCollister who delayed behind, for what we could not tell.

But he soon called after us, and swore he had enlisted a man fairly; but the man positively denied it.

McCollister, however, persisted in declaring that he had given him money, and enlisted him in due form.

"Well," says the sergeant, "you must go along with us and be sworn in, or else we must tie you and take you by force."

I do not recollect the time when my feelings were more hurt than on this occasion; the poor man was evidently trepanned, for McCollister put half a joe between his fingers and so offering his hand to the countryman under pretense of shaking hands with him, and the poor man giving his hand without any mistrust, McCollister said, "Take this in the name of the Congress of the United States," which frightened the simple rustic almost out of his senses.

We all marched on together, but did not go far before the poor man began to cry, and beg to be discharged, saying, "I have a wife and six small children, who must suffer if you take me from them. I will give you my horse, my saddle and great coat, and all the money I have, if you will let me return home."

Says the sergeant, "How much money do you have?"

"I have six dollars and some pence," replies the man, "with which I intended to have bought shoes for my children."

Upon this a consultation was held, and I pleaded as hard for the man as if he had been my own father. At length the sergeant consented and let him keep his horse, saddle and great coat and some of the money to bear his expenses home; and accordingly he departed congratulating himself on his happy delivery.

I have enlisted many a man, but I always despised the dishonest methods practiced by some of trepanning a man when he is intoxicated, and enlisting him by slipping a piece of money into his hand or into his pocket or into his boots and then swearing that he is enlisted fairly. If the devil does not get such recruiting officers, and all who follow such diabolical practices, I will give up that there is no occasion for a devil at all.

Shortly after this I was made a drill corporal, and from that a lance sergeant, and sent out recruiting. In this business I had tolerable success, and my captain, who was a man of good principles, would never enlist a man unless he was sober, and perfectly willing, and to this purpose he gave pointed orders to enlist every man fairly, as it was his opinion that a man so enlisted would be more likely to make a good soldier.

"For what," he would frequently say, "can you expect a

man to do for you when he is forced to it in an unlawful manner."

Before we leave Carlisle, a few desultory remarks on the town and the inhabitants may not be unacceptable to some of my readers.—Carlisle is a handsome town, regularly laid off in squares.[6] The courthouse is of brick and the market house of the same.

The Presbyterian meetinghouse is a spacious and elegant building of blue limestone, which makes a very beautiful appearance. There is also an Episcopal church built of stone, and the private homes are generally of stone and brick, with a few framed and log houses.

The university is a large and stately fabric and well calculated to answer the laudable purpose for which he was intended.[7]

When it was finished, the founders of this great building were at a loss for water:—a bletonist was procured, who pitched upon a certain spot of ground where they dug, and blew to a vast depth without finding water. They then procured a large auger which bored a hole four inches in diameter, with which they perforated the rock to a depth of 20 or 30 feet, and no prospect of water yet appeared.

A cube was then prepared, and a cartridge made to hold 20 pounds of the best powder, with which the hole was loaded, and fire applied.—The force of the explosion went both up and down, and the rock was so cleft and divided, that an immense body of water issued forth sufficient for the supply, not only for the university but of all the neighboring houses that stood in need of water.

The wells which are dug here are mostly deep: it being commonly necessary to penetrate through a very thick stratum of limestone rock. The usual depth of the wells is from 40 to 80 feet.

There are, however, many excellent springs in the vicinity

of Carlisle; such as Wilson's spring, which sends forth a stream sufficient to turn a mill at a very little distance from the source, and runs by the town in a considerable brook.[8]

And on the other side of the town is the river Conagoguin,[9] on the bank of which is a vast cave curiously formed by the hand of nature, with a spring on each side of it yielding the purest water. There is in this cavern about 100 yards from the entrance an elegant apartment of a square figure, large and spacious, and having seven beautiful boiling springs in the middle of it. In this room I have enjoyed a good deal of pleasure, and helped to drink many a good bottle.

The barracks are large enough to contain 10,000 soldiers, with a house convenient for 100 artificers to work in making all sorts of arms and implements for the use of the army and garrison.

The inhabitants of Carlisle are, generally speaking, of Irish extraction, and more particularly those who dwell in the main or back streets. They are very decent and respectable people. But there is a street very properly denominated Hell Street inhabited chiefly by high Dutch people, and in this street was kept the "holy" ground, where all sorts of pastimes were carried on.

From Carlisle we were ordered to Lancaster, in order to relieve the Congress regiment and to do duty over the prisoners who were taken with Cornwallis. We lay for some time in several old stables that had been occupied by the light horse; and afterwards formed into barracks, between Lancaster and Conestoga.[10] Here we mounted an officers guard—2 sergeants, 2 corporals, one drum and fife, and 50 privates, to guard the English prisoners, the magazine and the repository of provisions.

Here I cannot help mentioning a scene that I was witness to, though I acknowledge that it was something extraordinary and to me very unaccountable.

There is a hole in the ground on one side of the barracks,

called Stophel Funk's hole, that never could be closed; for if it was filled up in the evening, it would be filled up again in the morning; and old Funk would come forth several times at night, in the shape of a ball of fire.

One night in particular as we were going around with a relief and having stopped to relieve the sentinel next the grave-yard, who would come forth but old Funk in his usual appearance. I took the fire in my hands and threw it on the ground without receiving any hurt.

You may think what you please about it, I was frightened considerably, and all who were with me were glad to get to the guardhouse as quickly as possible; leaving the sentry in a trembling condition, who afterward gave us a sad account of old Funk. I have known the sentry to run from his post, from the magazine to the stores, in the greatest trepidation, panic-struck by the formidable appearance of old Funk.

And some who had courage enough to face the enemy in the field of battle, immediately took to their heels on the appearance of old Funk. Some asserted that they had seen him as a boy, others like a horse without a head, and others again as a wool-pack rolling on the ground; but for my part I never saw him in any other shape than that of a ball of fire.

The credibility of this incident will, no doubt, be questioned by many, and ascribed to prejudice, ignorance or superstitious credulity; but what I have seen and felt I must believe; and contenting myself with a faithful relation of the fact, I leave it to the philosopher, who may probably be able to account for the phenomenon, without having any recourse to any supernatural means.

We had to keep a quarter guard at the back of our barracks, which mounted a sergeant, corporal and 12 privates. It so happened that one time when I was on guard the sergeant, whose name was Pendergrass, sent me to call the relief, as I was then a corporal. At the same time he gave the prisoners leave to go and stay in the barracks, though contrary to orders; and then absented himself from the guard.

So between the hours of 11 and 12 at night the officer of the police, whose name was Ball, came round, and called for the sergeant of the guard; but the sergeant being absent, he called for the corporal of the guard; but no corporal was there to answer. He then called for the guard to fall in; but no guard; not a man was there but the sentry.

Lt. Ball then called for the sergeant-major of the regiment; but the sergeant was in bed with his wife, and I was not far from mine. But on hearing the sergeant-major called for, I began to call for No1, No. 2, No. 3, No. 4; and at the second call for the sergeant-major by the officer of the police, I called again as loud as I could bawl, No. 1, No. 2, No. 3, No. 4, in order to make it appear that I was on my duty.

But a new guard was called out, and you may easily guess what came next:—we were all confined under the new quarter guard for five days and nights from our wives; but I hope they did not suffer by our absence; for a soldier (to his honor be it spoken) is always ready to act a brotherly part in such a case as this.

On the fifth day a court martial was called, and the sergeant and myself were conveyed to the courthouse to be tried by a regimental court martial, according to the military law.—I was called into the room, "Corporal Shaw, you are charged with absenting yourself from your guard without leave—guilty or not guilty?"

"Not guilty; for please your honors, by the sergeant's own confession, I was in the line of my duty, as will no doubt appear, if your honors will confer the favor of calling in the sergeant."

So the sergeant was called in.

"Sergeant Pendergrass, was corporal Shaw absent from his guard with leave or without leave?"

"I sent corporal Shaw," said the sergeant, "to call a relief."

"What relief?"

"The first relief."

"Well," says the officer of the police, "I heard corporal Shaw call No. 1, No. 2, No. 3, No. 4 when I called the sergeant-major."

So I was dismissed into the next room. And the court proceeded to the trial of the sergeant; and when that was ended, we were conducted back to the guardhouse; and the next day at roll call the prisoners were brought out and a circle formed, and the sentence of the court martial was read. "Sergeant Pendergrass, you are broken, and to receive 50 lashes. Corporal Shaw, you are acquitted with honor, and may return to your duty."

In a short time sergeant Everly was cashiered for drunkenness, and I was made sergeant in his place. Not long after this, I was ordered out, in company with sergeant Smith (commonly called old-fashioned Smith) to go and bring back a deserter, who was harbored in a certain man's house in Pickway.[11]

We accordingly set out and pursued our search until we grew hungry, and having no money with which to bear our expenses, we were obliged to do the best we could—appear great and talk big—.

It was our lot to call at a tory's house and the man seemed all in confusion at our appearance, and very readily put down his bottle, and treated us with plenty of cider, and directed his wife to get ready the best in the house.

The conversation was soon turned upon whig and tory, and we had a plain indication of the truth of the good old proverb that "a guilty conscience needs no accuser." However, the old man through fear and not love treated us with much civility. We ate and drank freely, telling him that the congress would pay for all; and we gave him an order on congress, which he readily accepted, saying it would pay his taxes.

We parted in friendship with our host, having our canteens

filled with good old apple brandy, and pursued our journey, and made some inquiry for the deserter; but hearing that we were in search of him, he made his escape, and we gave over our pursuit.

In our return to Lancaster we called at the Sign of the Pennsylvania Farmer, a public house kept by a certain Crawford, about 10 miles from Lancaster and 56 miles from Philadelphia. Mr. Crawford was a true whig, who had warmly espoused the American cause;—he treated us with great hospitality and entertained us with the best his house would afford; not forgetting to fill our canteens, as he knew that a soldier loves to wet his whistle.

We then proceeded on our way for some distance and the day being far spent, we called for quarters at a certain Mr. H---'s near Lancaster.—Though the master of the house was not at home, we were nevertheless invited in, and treated with particular attention, for I was always of that principle, that I would not kiss the maid when I could kiss the mistress; but both, rather than be called nice.

We passed the night much to our satisfaction and got a good breakfast in the morning with a bumper of Jamaica spirits to wash it down; and so after eating and drinking heartily, we took our farewell of our kind hostess and returned to Lancaster in high spirits, and made a report of the manner in which we had endeavored to execute our orders.

In a few days I was sent on guard to the jail over the British prisoners. The jailor's name was C----; he had one son and three daughters. His old wife used to scare every guard that was on duty; for it was a common practice then to convey liquor to the prisoners, and the jailor exacted such an exorbitant price for his liquor that the soldiers were not able to buy it.

Being upon guard, application was made to me to procure some liquor on lower terms, and convey it to the prisoners. — Accordingly I undertook the task, and having procured a bladder, I took the wood out of my cartridge box and filled it with a half gallon of whiskey, and went up to the iron gate (without suspicion, as I thought) in order to hand in the liquor, when, to my great surprise, old Mrs. Devil-catcher cries out, "Oh, have I caught you!"

"What do you mean, madam?" said I.

"I will have you under guard, you scoundrel," said she. "I will go and complain to captain T---."

"Stop, madam," said I. "I will save you the trouble;" and at the same time very artfully called for my little book, and like a conjurer began to draw a magical circle in the barroom, saying, "I will fix you, my old lady."

Upon this, as she was a firm believer in the vulgar stories of ghosts, goblins and spectres, she was greatly alarmed and cried out, "O dear sentry, do not give him his little book!"

She then began to flatter me, promising me that I should never want for anything, whenever I mounted guard. So at her entreaties, I desisted from my conjuration, and made friends with my old mistress C.

My next object was to get on the right side of the eldest daughter, and this I accomplished in the following manner: having reason to believe that she had an intrigue with a certain Mr. T., I took the opportunity, when the young lovers had an interview at a certain time of the night, of presenting myself at the foot of the stairs, so as just to let myself be known by Mr. T., and then retired to my apartment.

The next morning when the family were dispersed about their different avocations, at a convenient time, I thus addressed Miss C.:

"Good morning, Miss, how did you rest last night?"

"Indeed, Mr. Shaw," said she, "I rested very badly, for I was troubled with ugly dreams all night."

"For my part, Miss," said I, "I was so terrified by an apparition that I was very near breaking the jail and clearing myself; but the sentry prevented me by telling me that nothing was more common than to hear a noise in the jail and see spirits. Besides, my fears were considerably abated, when I summoned up resolution enough to look at the apparition, and recognized the image that presented itself before me."

"Bless me, Mr. Shaw," she said with apparent concern, "and do you think you would know the person?"

"Yes, madam," said I, "it was the ghost of Mr. T. in full shape, holding by the hand one of the most beautiful creatures that my eyes ever beheld."

"Lord bless me, Mr. Shaw. You startle me! But do you think you would know the figure?"

"Yes, madam," said I. "It would represent your own fair image, if I mistake not. But I may possibly have mistaken it; for I absented myself as quickly as I could."

"Too true, indeed, Mr. Shaw, to make a joke of," answered she. "But I hope you will have honour enough in you to not make it known to the family."

"I would scorn such an action, madam," said I, but— but—

But from this time forth, having the old jade and her daughter both fearful of giving me offense, I fared very well, and could carry liquor, or anything else I pleased to the poor prisoners, without any danger of opposition or detection.

Chapter 5

"Arrah by my shoul, this tea makes all our men drunk, so it doss."

L ate in the summer of 1783 a second revolt took place among the soldiers of the Pennsylvania line.[1] The ring-leaders were sergeant major Morris and sergeant Noggle, both belonging to the 3d Pennsylvania regiment.

They were to march on to join their confederates at Phila-delphia; but as soon as the regiment had commenced their march, sergeant major Morris deserted and left us in the lurch.

He lay concealed, as it later appeared, in Chamberstown.[2]

This plot was concerted and kept with the greatest secrecy amongst the non-commissioned officers; though it was never communicated to me until the day appointed for putting it in execution arrived.

I was at work with a certain Mr. Myers in Lancaster, when I was alarmed by a message from sergeant Noggle, desiring me to come and join the regiment on their march, and that they had appointed me captain of a company. But I very positively refused it, and said I was pointedly opposed to all such unlawful traitorous conspiracies against the government of the United

States; adding that I was perfectly satisfied with the treatment that I had received from my superior officers; for they were men of the first respectability, and of as sound principles as could be found on the continent.

This answer I returned to my new commanders; but a second message was sent to me, with orders to bring me either by flattery or by force.

So at length I yielded and went, at the request of sergeant Noggle and served as a private soldier, during our absence from Lancaster. We marched a few miles out of town where we encamped the first night; and Lt. Butler was sent to us offering any reasonable satisfaction, and promising that all arrearages would be paid up if we would return to our duty.

But we were still fed up by Noggle's fine stories of what would be done for us at Philadelphia. Accordingly, we marched on, and entered the city in three days, with drums beating and colours flying and all in good order. We halted a little until a council was held by all the non-commissioned officers in the army.

A plan was accordingly laid, and a guard sent to seize the magazines. The next day all the forces were collected and marched to the state house where sergeant Noggle made a speech representing at large our grievances, such as no pay— no clothing, nor other necessities and conveniences, without which we could serve no longer. And the majority of the soldiers protested they would not leave the ground before they obtained full satisfaction or took the congress prisoners by surrounding the state house.

And I myself saw a soldier by the name of Wright charge on one of the members of congress with his bayonet, while the gentleman was on his escape, after promising to do everything in his power to have the arrearages of pay and clothing paid off.

At the same time, thousands of citizens were crying, "Stand for your rights."

The city militia with several troops of light horse were called out to disband us by force; but they would not obey their commanders,—and the general voice was "Stand for your rights."

Messengers were sent to inform us that measures would be immediately taken for redressing all our grievances; and having received satisfactory assurances of this, we all marched to the barracks, and from thence the 3d Pennsylvania regiment marched back to Lancaster.

Old col. Humpton was placed at Hogden's ferry, with such clothing as we stood in need of, and some money. So we continued our march under the command of lt. Talbot, and when we arrived at Lancaster, we were formed in a line on the parade, and were ordered to lay down our arms, and the ringleaders of the plot were selected out.

Accordingly, sergeant Noggle, corporal Flowers, and some others, were sent to the jail in Lancaster; from thence they were afterwards removed to Philadelphia jail, where was also lt. Huston, who had been taken up on suspicion.—General Washington also sent a guard in pursuit of sergeant-major Morris, who was taken and brought to Philadelphia and there tried by a general court martial for mutiny. Both he and sergeant Noggle were sentenced to be shot; but while they were on their knees, and the cap drawn over their faces, and the soldiers waiting for the word "fire" through the great clemency of General Washington a reprieve was obtained, and the prisoners discharged, to the entire satisfaction of all the spectators.

Soon after this event we were all discharged at Lancaster, and received four months' pay in Morris's notes payable in 60 days, with all the arrearages of clothing, and after some time we got continental certificates; and I got 350 acres of land as extra pay for my services.

Whilst the money lasted we lived merrily; but that being soon squandered, my comrade and myself entered into a contract with one lawyer Clymer to dig him a mill race by Morgantown, on the horseshoe road, 24 miles from Lancaster. And as this work employed us for a considerable time, I left my bedfellow at home, hoping that she would not suffer, as one soldier is always ready to help another in time of need.

We had not been long at work before we became acquainted wih the overseer, whose name was John Oatencake, who frequently led us to a certain tavern in Morgantown to spend leisure evenings; and there was a handsome landlady, and bucksome young damsel who loved a game of cards and was tolerably expert, particularly at the game of all-fours, in playing which, however, we were always so generous as to stake three to one, considering our purses the heaviest; but they contrived to lighten them before we had done with them.

After finishing the mill race, we returned to Lancaster, and in a week or two, we started for Philadelphia, by a circuitous route, that is to say, by way of Peddlehouzer,[3] to Pickway, to the Gap tavern, down Newport road[4] to Irwin's, thence to Cochran's, to the halfway house in Chester county, and so on to New London crossroads, where our money failed, and we called at a farmer's house to enquire for work; he readily agreed to give us two shillings a day to top corn.

This was a business with which I was entirely unacquainted; so that at the first attempt, there was a boy of 12 years of age, who soon left me behind. But before night I improved so far as to undo both the farmer and his son.

Having stayed with the farmer a few days, we left him and proceeded on to Newark, [Delaware] and from thence to Christian Bridge,[5] where we fell in with one Dr. M., a man of good repute, who gave us employment for some time, and treated us well. But at length we were obliged to leave the place for—for—for doing what we could not help doing.—

We next pursued our journey to Wilmington; thence to

Chester, and from that to Darby, and so on to the city of Philadelphia.

Two companies were then being raised for the purpose of dispossessing the Yankees of the town of Wyoming.[6] These companies were raised by the captains Stoddard and Christie; we joined them and shortly after marched forth, under the command of major Moore, who conducted the expedition.

We marched on through Germantown, Easttown, [Easton] crossed the Schuylkill,[7] and passed the White Oak run, and so on through the wilderness to Wyoming, and took Fort Dickinson on the river Susquehanna. After we had been there some time, a proclamation was issued out ordering the Yankees to remove from Wyoming, Kingston, and Shawneetown; and all places on the disputed lands before spring or abide by the consequences.

That winter we received orders to open a road through the wilderness; and in our course we met with a place called the Shades of Death,[8] on which the sun is not seen to shine the whole year round. And as we were employed in making a bridge over a rivulet, I was severely frost-bitten for the first time.

The road being finished, we returned to Wyoming, where I met with another singular misfortune, by which my life was in great danger.—

By an unlucky accident, I got my shoulder displaced, and on my recovery I went down to the river side for recreation. There happened to be a Spaniard fishing in the river, by the side of a canoe, and he got his line tangled at the stern of the canoe, and went into it to loose the line; and I very inconsiderately stepped into the canoe also.

At the same time there chanced to be a soldier on the bank who was a funny old fellow, and he pushed off the canoe for his diversion; but his ill-timed fun had like to have terminated my existence; for the Spaniard being awkward and myself lame, we were in no condition to manage the canoe, which having floated with us a short distance overset, and turned us into the water, to shift for ourselves.

We had a hard struggle; sometimes up and sometimes down. This I call a fair sea fight between the English and the Spanish. However, the Spaniard kept the ship, and the Englishman ran aground; for I luckily gained the shore by swimming, whereas the Spaniard stuck to the canoe; but no thanks to him for his perseverance; for he was tied to his quarter-tiers; there being a rope with a stone, for a cable and anchor at the head of the canoe.

In the scuffle he accidentally got the rope fastened around his legs, and therefore having no chance to run away, he must either fight or die by his vessel. The canoe carried him down for a considerable way, when by good fortune, a boat, coming up the river, he was extricated from danger and his life preserved.

About this time some expectation being entertained of receiving pay, a merchant in the town of Wyoming, who had some damaged goods on his hands, proposed to let the soldiers have what they wanted upon bringing an order from the captain; and accordingly we took up goods whenever we thought proper.

Amongst other articles in the store there was a considerable quantity of tea, of which the soldiers would occasionally get three or four pounds at a time, and go to one captain Hollowback's and barter the tea for whiskey; so that it became a pretty common practice to return home reeling, like the drunken soldier, who being ordered to "wheel to the right;"

"By gad," says he, "I wheel every way, and some must be right."

On these occasions, there was a certain Molly McNight, an old sergeant's wife, upon seeing the soldiers come staggering into the garrison, would say, "Arrah by my shoul, this tea makes all our men drunk, so it doss."

John R. Shaw as a
prodigal.

For my part, I went to captain Hollowback's still-house one
day with two of my fellow soldiers and having called for a quart
of whiskey, we drank it before the fire. But upon attempting to
rise, with an intention of returning to the barracks, I fell down
motionless, and to all appearances dead; so that the alarm went
to the barracks that Shaw was dead.

A company then collected to my wake, and having procured a good keg of whiskey, were determined to have a merry frolic: but they were sadly disappointed; for as soon as the operation of the liquor began to abate, I rolled off the board upon which they had laid me, and uttered a heavy groan, accompanied by a loud explosion of flatus from beneath, which so startled the company that they all ran out swearing that the dead was come to life.

However, they soon returned, and conveyed me to the barracks, where I was seized with a fit of insanity, and behaved in such an outrageous manner that they were obliged to confine me with chains and take off my clothes.

But by some means I got loose, and ran through the fort like a Bedlamite, climbed up to the top of the roof of the barracks, and walking to the farther end ridge, jumped down without any injury and ran out of the garrison until I came to the cliffs by the side of the river, from whence I leaped down (the distance not being less than 30 or 40 feet) to the bottom, seated myself on a cake of ice, and floated for a considerable distance down the river before my fellow soldiers could get me off.

I was then taken care of, and doctored up with a little more of the usquebaugh, which in the condition I then was, produced no bad effects, but seemed rather to contribute to the restoration of my health and the recovery of my senses.

Chapter 6

"We jogged on to the sign of the Battle of the Cags."

At the breaking up of the ice, the towns of Kingston and Wyoming were considerably damaged by an inundation of the river. The water rose to an astonishing height; the ice having broken up between 11 and 12 o'clock at night.

So impetuous was the current and so sudden the overflow, that it was with no small difficulty the men in the fort, or even the inhabitants of the place could make their escape; for the water was up to our knees before we got off.

We then fled to the hills for safety. I there saw houses floating down the river, with cocks crowing in them, and cattle of every description descending with the stream.

Kingston was entirely swept away—not a house was left in the town, but a barn on one side. All the cattle were drowned; and our commissary, whose name was Meeds, being of a roguish turn, and wishing to profit by the losses of others, collected all the drowned cattle and hogs, and salted them up for the use of the army.

But when his dishonesty was discovered, he very deservedly lost his commission and another commissary was appointed in his stead.

While we continued here I went one day into the woods to cut down some timber; and it so happened that one tree which I was endeavoring to bring to the ground was prevented from falling by lodging in the fork of another tree. I was brought to a stand what method to take in order to get it down.

At length, however, I concluded to use the following contrivance; I suspended the axe at the waistband of my breeches, and then crawled up the tree which was lodged, with more clumsiness than a bear, and thus with great difficulty I gained the top, where I cut off the smallest branch of the fork; but I cannot tell whether the tree, the axe, or myself were on the ground first, so sudden was the downfall.

For I flung my arms around the standing tree, but not getting such a firm hold as to support me, I necessarily came down with the falling tree; and by the friction against the rough bark of the standing tree, I got my body as well shaved as the best barber in the world could have done it.

As soon as I recovered from the trepidation occasioned by the suddenness of this accident, I proceeded to trimming the branches of the tree, which in its fall had bent down some pretty stiff saplings, and having inconsiderately cut off the top of one of them, which I mistook for a branch of the tree, it rebounded with force and struck me so violently on the mouth that it laid me sprawling.

I rolled over and over and over, until I got on my posteriors, where I sat for a little while like a baboon, looking around me, to observe if there was any person beholding me in that awkward posture.

But now for the Yankees.—Our general orders were, if they did not voluntarily remove, to drive them off by force. Our two companies were divided into small parties and commanded to go round and take off the locks of the Yankees' guns. Major

Moore then issued orders that they should depart within the space of ten days, as no longer indulgence could be allowed them.

These orders, however, were not complied with and accordingly at the expiration of the time, the small parties went round the second time, and drove off all the inhabitants of both town and country that would not consent to live under the Pennsylvania laws.

The sight was truly affecting, and sufficient to excite pity in the most insensible breasts, to behold men, women, and children driven into the woods without being permitted to carry with them any clothing except what was on their backs.

It made my heart ache to see wives weeping round their husbands, and poor little helpless children crying, and hanging on their afflicted mothers; and in this condition driven into the remotest part of the desert, where they must be exposed to the greatest hardships and dangers without any prospect of relief.

Some time in the month of April, 1784, this land was divided into lots and small farms, and offered to those who would take it under the laws of Pennsylvania. Accordingly, some of the soldiers took lots and some farms, from the hands of squire Patterson, who was appointed agent for the state of Pennsylvania. Each man had to pay one ear of corn per acre to be considered as a tax for the land.

We were all paid off and discharged in the month of May, and there were 19 of us who immediately set out together for the city of Philadelphia. We marched on to the White Oak run (32 miles from Wyoming and 34 miles from Easttown) [Easton] where we stopped a few hours to refresh ourselves, and made up a shooting match and shot for three gallons of whiskey, 30 yards at a large stump four feet over, and it accidentally happened that I proved the best marksman.

A very melancholy event had occurred here the night

before we arrived; a poor man who had a wife and two children was gone a hunting;—the night was very cold, and they were extremely ill-provided with clothes—the mother had to get up in the night and put warm stones to her children's feet, but notwithstanding, both the mother and her children were found frozen to death the next morning.[1]

After seeing the remains of these unhappy victims of poverty decently interred, we pursued our journey toward East-town, 12 miles from Bethlehem; and when we arrived there we purchased a boat to carry us down the Delaware to Philadelphia.

We were now arrived in one of the finest and most plentiful cities in the world. The first thing I did was to enquire for such persons as bought continental soldiers' pay, and I soon found a certain McConnel, to whom I sold mine. My pay and my 350 acres of land brought me 63 pounds 6 shillings.

The next thing was to spend this money, and with this in view I immediately repaired to the Sign of the Checkers or Draughts in Water street,[2] and there I fell in with two sailors whom I invited to drink some grog, and began to be so obstreperous and to cut so many capers that the landlady was obliged to beg me to be less noisy, observing that she had a sick man in the house, and that it would be cruel and inhuman to disturb him in such a condition.

The sailors then asked me if I wanted to have a frolic. I answered yes, provided we can get a suitable place, and some fine girls to amuse us.—We then jogged on to the Sign of the Battle of the Cags.

But as it is possible that some of my readers may not have heard of the battle of the cags, I will give them a brief explanation of it. While the British army were in possession of Philadelphia, the Americans sent a considerable number of empty barrels or cags down the river Delaware. The British suspecting these vessels to contain some combustible matter for the destruction of the city, drew up their forces in battle array, and commenced a formidable discharge of artillery upon these empty cags.

But they soon discovered their mistake, and withdrew the fight, and marched off to their quarters with shame and disgrace, for being outwitted by men born in the woods.[3] The Americans in this instance acted somewhat like those seamen who, when they meet a whale, immediately fling him out an empty barrel by way of amusement to divert him from damaging the ship.

By having arrived at the Sign of the Cags, the landlady with a smiling and inviting countenance taking me by the hand, says to me in a pleasant and courteous manner, "Will this room answer your purpose; for I understand you wish to have a frolic."

"Yes, madam," said I, "with another small apartment for greater convenience."

I accordingly agreed with the old lady for the room, and the different prices of the liquors, and the next thing was to make choice of company suitable to the occasion.

The old lady then sent for half a dozen brisk lassies de bonne humeur, with as many sailors and soldiers, and an old fiddler to compose our jovial party. We soon had our ballroom in complete order, and commenced our frolic late in the evening and passed the night agreeably enough.

In such scenes of wild festivity, in the company of the most profligate and debauched characters, I continued until all my money was spent; and then to work I had to go.

I met with a certain Charles West, a Quaker, who employed me to dig a cellar for him, in company with one Miller, a Scotchman, who was as full of vanity and folly as myself.

But it would be abusing your patience, my dear reader, to trouble you with a detail of my numerous frolics and irregularities while I remained in the city of Philadelphia. Suffice it to say that every penny I made by my work was immediately squandered away in the haunts of dissipation and vice.

I got so far, however, in favor with the good Quaker that he recommended me to one George Justice, a bricklayer, who employed me in carrying the hod, and in this branch of business I soon became as expert as any in the city. I have run down six men in a day, in carrying the hod up houses from two to six stories high; indeed I never saw a man in my life but I could outwind him.

For this reason, my employer always gave me extra wages, to push every man that came to carry bricks.

Among others employed in this work there was an Irishman by the name of Jemmy; and our employer one time in particular sent for some beer to treat his hands with. After we had all drunk round, and Jemmy and myself had carried a few hods of brick, "Arrah, by my shoul," says Jemmy, "this beer will all die, master Justice."

"Well, Jemmy," says Mr. Justice, "thou mayest drink it, if thou thinkest proper."

So Jemmy took a hearty drink of it. But behold, after carrying a few more bricks, down came Jemmy, hod and all! The house was three stories high, and poor Jemmy took up his quarters in the cellar, from which he was obliged to be conveyed in a carriage, with his shoulder out of place and his head sorely bruised. And so much for drinking beer.

I continued with Mr. Justice until some time in the month of August (1784) when the first American regiment was raised, commanded by colonel Josiah Harmar, and consisted of four companies for Fort McIntosh,[4] 35 miles below Pittsburgh on the Ohio, on the Indian side.

Having still a predelection for the military life, I enlisted in captain William McCurdy's company. The officers of the four companies were major Finney, and the captains St. Clair, McCurdy and Douglas.

About a month after I enlisted, my former employer, who had reluctantly parted with me, wanted to buy me off, and after some persuasion, he prevailed on me to go and try to obtain the captain's consent; which I did and offered him two men in my place and twenty dollars in cash.

But he answered, "No, Shaw, I cannot part with you, for I have just spoken to colonel Harmar to make you a corporal."

To tell the truth, I was very easy about it, for I loved the life of a soldier. The bounty indeed was so small that it could not be sufficient inducement to any man to enlist who was not otherwise inclined to it; for we had but two dollars in advance and one complete suit of clothes. A soldier's pay was 50 shillings per month, a corporal's 55 shillings, a sergeant's ten dollars and a sergeant major's fifteen dollars.—No stoppages, however, for the doctor, nor for the chaplain, as in the English army; but every man had liberty to practice physic and pray for himself.

After we had been recruiting for some time, we formed a camp on the side of the Schuylkill opposite to the city, and occasionally were permitted to go into the city, by procuring a pass, or a non-commissioned officer to answer for our conduct and bring us back at roll call in the evening.

In these walks we usually passed over Mr. Hogden's floating bridge at the middle ferry. But one day as a certain corporal Vaughan and myself were deliberately walking over this bridge, not thinking of any obstruction, as we had often gone over before unmolested, old Mr. Hogden attacked us on the bridge, and demanded pay for crossing, and asked us for our pass.

Upon this I shewed him my fist as he advanced seemingly with an intent to strike me, and I gave him such a blow on the ear as laid him asleep for a little while.

In the meantime the son came to the old man's assistance and my comrade soon gave him what Paddy gave the drum— more kicks than coppers. After that, we could pass over the bridge without interruption or molestation.

As soon as we had gained a sufficient number of men, we received orders to march; and after we had marched about 13 miles (to the Sign of the Sorrel Horse) we halted for one day and two nights, as there was something to be done there. Some of the men had deserted and were taken—they belonged to Captain St. Clair's company. They were tried and two of them were sentenced to run the gauntlet, three times through. One of them died that night by the severity of the punishment; and the other eloped and was never heard of more.

Captain St. Clair, though an officer of an undeniable character, was in some instances too severe. He has wished many times to get me into his clutches.

His mode of punishment for petty crimes was flagellation, performed by laying the offender across a bench with his back upwards, and causing his corporal to stand by, with a ratan in his hand, which he ludicrously styled his washerwoman.

"Now," he would say, "you must give my holy angel a few dozen on his bare posteriors, to enable him to remember his old friend St. Clair."

This officer was too cunning for most of his soldiers; but at length he was outwitted by one William Grub. The captain's horse being sick, he applied to Grub, who was something of a farrier, to cure his horse.

Accordingly Grub having examined the horse and found that his back was sore, and severely bruised, returned to the captain and told him he would undertake the cure provided he (St. Clair) would supply him with the medicine.

The captain, finding that it was nothing more than a bottle of whiskey readily granted it.

So Grub and one of his comrades went to work upon the horse, and having rubbed his back with the bottle and poured a few drops on the sore, they both set down very contentedly and drank the whiskey.

"And now," said they, "we have outgeneralled the old fellow."

But being overheard, word went immediately to the captain who, upon finding himself so easily outdone, offered another bottle to any person who would discover to him the trick.

Upon this Grub himself came forward and told him that he had rubbed the horse's back with the bottle and drank the contents. The captain then treated him with another bottle and laughed heartily at the joke.

From the Sign of the Sorrel Horse where we had stopped as is mentioned above, we marched on to Lancaster, and encamped on the Conestoga,[5] where we drew provisions, and continued one day. From thence we marched on to Carlisle; and from Carlisle to Shippensburg, where we flogged two men for desertion. From Shippensburg we proceeded to Chambersburg, and here we flogged one man for desertion and drummed him out with a rope about his neck.

The next day we marched to Bedford, where we halted for several days. And for the first night, 12 of us got liberty to stay in the town, and we put up at the Sign of the Blazing Star.

Among our jolly company was one corporal Cragg, a man of a remarkably funny turn. Whilst we were drinking by a good fireside, this Mr. Cragg (who commonly went by the name of Honour Bright that always scorns the clean thing) says with a serious countenance, at the same time rubbing his beard and looking up the chimney at some hams of bacon, "I will have you off bright and early."

The landlady supposing that he meant to shave his beard, for it was then very long, told him there was no razor in the house. Cragg, however, wanted not the razor, but the hams of bacon; and accordingly as soon as the family were asleep, he took the opportunity and very slyly bore off the bacon with him. So much for Cragg.

As for myself, I and another brother toper got so intoxicated that we could not confine ourselves to the house; but rambled through the town ready for mischief. The first thing that happened in our way was a garden fence, which we pulled down, and let the cows, horses and sheep into the garden to destroy the contents.

We then proceeded on in search of adventures until our mad career was terminated by my falling into a well 20 feet deep, where I lay until I was drawn out by the assistance of major John McGaughey, now resident in Shelbyville, [Kentucky] and fortunately received no damage.

The next day four men composing what we called the Irish Mess, viz. Connor, Welch, Hannan and Sands, went to a certain store in the town, and the storekeeper having occasion to go into another apartment, these fellows entered and began to plunder the store, and when the storekeeper returned Mr. Connor instantly knocked him down, while the rest were busied in pillaging the goods.

But the town being alarmed, the ruffians were taken by the sheriff and lodged in the jail; and as soon as the intelligence reached the ears of the commanding officer of the troops he sent a guard for them, and they were brought to the camp, and a drum-head court martial was held, by which they were sentenced to receive 100 lashes each. This punishment was inflicted, and so hardened were these villains in wickedness that they bore it with fortitude worthy of a better cause.

Chapter 7

"I could find people enough to take
a shilling out of my pocket . . ."

T he next day we marched for Hannahstown[1] and so on for
Pittsburgh, and we crossed the Allegheny at a small
island opposite Fort Pitt, and lay there for a short time,
until proper measures were taken for a treaty with the Indians.

We then marched down to Fort McIntosh, where we held a
treaty with four tribes of Indians.

It was my lot, in company with eight others, to be employed in boating goods for the treaty, and provisions for the
troops down the Ohio. Our first cargo, however, consisted of
cannon and ammunition, which we brought in a flat bottomed
boat belonging to a certain Mr. Elliot, and delivered at Fort
McIntosh (or at the mouth of Big Beaver creek).

We were then sent back with the boat, having on board Mr.
Elliot himself as passenger and we were four days arriving and
getting 35 miles, and drinking a barrel of whiskey. When we got
up to Pittsburgh another boat was put into our possession by
one captain O'Hara,[2] who was contractor for the army, and is
now resident in Pittsburgh.

In this boat we made four voyages; and on the fifth voyage three officers came on board, viz., Col. Harmar, Dr. McDowell and lieut. Bell. When these officers came on board I was considered as having no more command, but had to sit and row as a common person.

After having sailed about 18 or 20 miles, we put in to the shore for the night, and kept sentry in the boat. The next morning a large English cheese was missing, and great search was made for it. But at length a man by the name of Shicken found it in the river at the stern of the boat where in all probability he had put it himself.

But colonel Harmar swore that every man should be flogged when we arrived at Fort McIntosh; but it must be observed that he and the other officers were, if not intoxicated, at least highly inspired, for they drank freely.

We sailed about 2 o'clock and took the liberty of speaking to the steersmen several times and warning them of the danger we were in of striking against the rocks, at the same time intreating them to steer for the Virginia shore,[3] or every man would be lost. But the best word I could get from colonel Harmar was "Silence, you d----d rascal, or I will have you flogged for an example to the rest."

In a few minutes, however, the boat struck, and Mr. Shicken and myself jumped into the water, and bore the stern up the river, and I ordered two men to hold her in that position to prevent the boat from being overset.

You may judge now, my candid readers, how the tone was altered from "you d----d rascals" to "Now, my clever fellows, which of you will leap out and swim ashore and run down to Fort McIntosh and bring us another boat?"

The distance to the fort was about 10 miles, the river full of ice, and the banks covered with a deep snow. Notwithstanding the hazardous enterprise, I pulled off my coat, tied a hand-kerchief on my head, and taking a setting pole in my hand, I jumped into the river, and taking the advantage of the current till the water reached my breast, I swam about five or six hundred yards before I struck the bank.

Tom Shicken followed my example and landed safely. We then held a consultation, and judging that there was a house about four miles up the river we concluded to make for it, which we accordingly did, and to our great joy we found a canoe, and by the assistance of the owner we hauled her into the river, for she lay about 40 yards from the river.

We then proceeded down the river in a cold and shivering condition; our clothes were frozen stiff on our backs, but we were not gone more than two hours until we returned with the canoe.

Having arrived at the boat, we refreshed ourselves with some ardent spirits and then commenced unloading the boat. And from this time colonel Harmar from the most embittered enemy, became the most singular friend to me in every instance, as you will find in the sequel to this narrative.

As soon as we could get the boat off, we set in for the shore, where we left Dr. McDowell and two private soldiers to take care of the goods, which we could not carry with us, until we slipped down to the fort and returned for the balance of the lading.

Having tarried a few days to refresh ourselves, we sailed to Pittsburgh, by order of colonel Harmar, and waited there until captain O'Hara was ready to embark the balance of goods and provisions with which he had contracted to furnish the troops.

Having received our cargo, we set sail late in the afternoon, with an expectation of arriving at Fort McIntosh early the next morning. But we had to stop at Mr. Elliot's mill (three miles below Pittsburgh) for some barrels of flour.

At this time the ice was flowing in great abundance, and having been detained at the mill until 9 o'clock at night, it was with no small difficulty we got into the channel of the river. I

John R. Shaw, corporal in Captain McCurdy's company,
cast away.

had to stand on a plank about a foot broad, and steer the boat
(which was built after the manner of a batteau) but unluckily
the broad end of the oar slipped on a cake of ice, and the plank
on which I stood became slippery.

I pitched headlong into the river, and was out of sight for
some time; but a kind providence made way for me, and at
length I got my head above the ice, and some of the men in the
boat putting out a setting pole, I caught hold of it and was drawn
into the boat, and my life preserved.

As soon as I got into the boat captain O'Hara says to me,
"You had better go and pull the fore oar."

Accordingly, wet as I was, I obeyed his orders, and the
consequence was that I froze stiff in a few minutes.

The men wrought hard for about an hour endeavoring to
make their way through the ice; but at last the boat struck
against a fish-basket below the mouth of Shirtee on the Virginia
side, on the 22nd day of December, 1784.[4]

Here we lay all that night expecting death every moment;
and indeed had it not been for the iron on the stern of the boat,

which enabled her to withstand the shocks of the floating ice, we must inevitably have perished.

Even the recollection causes me to shudder, when I reflect how narrowly I escaped ending my misspent life. Every means in our power were used to dislodge the boat from the fish-basket. When a cake of ice would dash against the boat, every man that was able to stir would jump out, up to his neck in water, and exert himself to the utmost, but in vain.

While we lay in this distressed situation, our cries were heard to Pittsburgh. Captain O'Hara offered 200 guineas to any man who would bring him safe to the bank.

Induced by this offer, two men set out from the land in a canoe, with an axe and some fire; but they had not advanced above twice the length of their canoe before they were obliged to return to the bank, which they did with great difficulty, and to the imminent danger of their lives.

At length we came to a determination of throwing the lading overboard; but captain O'Hara was opposed to the measure, as part of the lading belonged to himself and part to the United States. Notwithstanding this, we had firmly resolved to throw overboard not only the cargo, but captain O'Hara himself, if he persisted in his opposition.

From the conduct of captain O'Hara in this instance it appeared that he cared very little for the lives of his men, provided he and his goods could be saved.

All hands then fell to lightening the boat until she floated down into the eddy under Magee's rocks,[5] and every man made the best of his way to the bank over the ice; except myself who lay not able to stir, with two men to keep me company, one by the name of Grub and the other of Shicken.

Those two men remained with me until about three hours before day, when they leaped up, and swore that the boat was going off, and immediately proceeded on the ice towards the bank; but they broke through the ice, and had it not been for some branches of a sycamore tree that extended over the bank, which they fortunately caught hold of, they would most probably have been lost.

I begged of them if there was a rope about the house where they were going, to send the ablest man, and tell him to tie it about my middle and drag me to the land. But word was soon brought me that there was no rope about the house. I then gave myself up for lost, expecting nothing but death; for had the boat gone off, she and myself must have inevitably have been dashed to pieces on the ice.

In this hopeless condition, I lay until the rising of the sun, when lo! to my inexpressible joy, the lieutenants Butler and Smith came to Mr. Wood's just below the mouth of Shirtee, and seeing all the men except myself, they made inquiry after me, and were told that the boat had been seen descending the river with me; but not being satisfied of the truth of the information, they proceeded to the head of Magee's rocks, where they beheld me lying in the boat.

Accordingly, with great humanity, and not without difficulty, they conveyed me to the shore, and lt. Butler carried me on his back up the cliff to Wood's house, and laid me before the fire, where I fainted immediately. Upon this, they put me between two feather beds, where I lay until a large tub of fresh spring water was prepared for me, when my feet and legs were put into it, which was no doubt beneficial, for I was frozen up to the knees.

A large poultice of turnips was afterwards applied to my feet and legs. Here I lay for 21 days in such a deplorable condition that I was expected to die every hour.

There are three men now living in Kentucky who were eyewitnesses to my sad misfortune, gentlemen of the first character, to whom any reader who is desirous of proving the truth of this relation may apply: viz. Mr. Rogers, Sr., of Bryan Station,[6] and John Rogers his son, and James Stephenson of

Madison county; for these gentlemen were (as I said before) eyewitnesses of my unhappy case.

When the river became navigable I was taken down in a boat belonging to a Mr. Hulen, to Fort McIntosh, and safely conveyed into the garrison, and put into the barracks room with sergeant-major Duffey, his wife and corporal Reed, next door to the apartment occupied by colonel Harmar and his lady.

Here I was accommodated with all sorts of necessities, with two orderly men to wait on me, and the attendance of two physicians, Dr. McDowell and Dr. Allison. In short, no assistance was wanting, which could be rendered to a human creature in my situation.

The kindness of Mrs. Harmar still remains fresh in my memory, and shall never be forgotten. She sent me every day the best viands, and the choicest liquors her table could afford; and everything suitable to a person in my weak and helpless condition. Indeed had I been a commissioned officer I could not have expected better treatment.

Before the termination of the winter a quarrel arose among several of the officers, and each company espousing the cause of their own officer, fell into the ranks, determined to die by the side of their respective captains. There would most probably have been bloody work, had it not been for the interference of major Finney, who threatened the offending officers with a prosecution if they did not desist from their hostile intentions. Captain McCurdy was immediately put under arrest. But how matters were compromised among the officers was never known by the private soldiers.

While we lay at Fort McIntosh, general orders were given that no soldier should have liberty to buy spiritous liquors without a permit in writing first obtained from a commissioned officer. Agreeably to these orders, a certain corporal Carney one day made application to his lieutenant for liberty to buy a quart of rum. This unfeeling officer, having a black thorn stick in his

John R. Shaw as a
soldier.

hand, made no more to do, but knocked out the poor corporal's
brains; and the consequence was, that the lieutenant was put
under arrest and sent up to Fort Pitt to be tried for wilful
murder.

But he was liberated and suffered to run at large by reason
of the regiments being disbanded, in consequence of the time
for which they enlisted being expired; so that there was no court
martial to try him, and what became of him afterwards I know
not.

During my stay there every exertion was made for my
recovery, and on the 19th day of August, 1785, at my request I

was discharged with two others, viz. John Harris and Thomas Parks as unfit for either field or garrison duty.

We were furnished with a recommendation to the honorable legislature of the state of Pennsylvania, in order to receive a pension allowed to soldiers in similar circumstances. We were accordingly sent to Fort Pitt in a boat, with orders to stay in the garrison as long as we pleased, and draw provisions, and when we set off for Philadelphia to draw one month's provisions to carry us there.

Being much lamer than the other two, I had to travel 300 miles upon crutches. And when we came to Annas-town,[7] we met two companies of three year's men; and the captain, who was from New England, being a soldier's friend, treated us with much politeness, and gave us some money to bear our expenses, and made intercession with some pack-horsemen to convey us to New Bedford,[8] which they agreed to do; and when we arrived there, we parted with them and proceeded on our journey for Philadelphia.

We saw very hard times until we came to Carlisle. Here being particularly acquainted with many of the citizens, I presented my discharge and recommendation to the magistrates of the town, who went about and raised money sufficient for our travelling expenses to the city of Philadelphia.

As soon as we arrived in the city we parted, and for my part I had but one 11-penny piece left; and I thought I must go where I had left many a half joe, which was at the Sign of the Globe, behind the barracks. The landlord's name was Sell.

Accordingly, assuming an air of self-importance, I went in boldly, and called for a quart of beer.

"O, how do you do, Mr. Shaw," says the landlord.

"Not very well, Mr. Sell; I have met with a bad misfortune, by being frostbitten, which I fear will occasion me a lameness for life."

I soon discovered the countenance of my landlord to

change; and he began to make excuses as not being able to help me, etc., without being asked.

So I took the hint, drank off my beer, and determined to try my fortune elsewhere. I then went to the Sign of the Half Moon, kept by a certain Mr. Apkey, above Pool's bridge, between Front and Second Streets; and made my case known to the landlord, and begged him to let me stay in his house for two or three weeks; telling him at the same time that I had no money, but was in hopes of getting a pension.

"Well, stranger," replied Mr. Apkey, "if you can put up with such fare as I have, you are welcome to my house."

In a few days I made application at the Orphan's Court; where were also several others on the same business. I employed a certain Mr. Barton, an attorney, to present my recommendation; but nothing could be done; for no provision had been made for such soldiers as were disabled since the revolutionary war.

My attorney then drew me a petition to the General Assembly, which I presented myself. It was read and ordered to be laid on the table, but in a few days I prevailed on one of the members to have it brought to a second reading; upon which a committee consisting of Mr. Creak, Mr. Clymer,[9] and Mr. Finley were appointed to consider my case. In a few days they met and reported. The result of which was that it would be better to petition the council.

A letter being given to me for that purpose, directed to Squire Shippen,[10] requesting of him to use his utmost endeavors in having the pension bill amended.

From Squire Shippen I went with a note to Squire Rush[11] and to another gentleman, requesting of them to meet at 4 in the evening of that day, which accordingly they did in company with colonel Harmar but without effecting anything of consequence, further than that of giving me a letter to the council, who promised that something should be done next session for me.

I thought it hard, but submitted with patience, placing my confidence in that Beneficent Being who always is willing and able to help all who call on him, as I fully experienced in Philadelphia when first I made application for my pension.

Being in want of the common support of nature, and not being able to work, ashamed to beg, and dreading the consequence of stealing—in this wretched situation, I one day sat on a wharf, bewailing my sad destiny, when a lad stepped up to me, saying,

"Stranger, what is your complaint? And what has brought you to this distress? Tell me freely and I will afford you all the relief that is in the power of a 'prentice boy."

I told him that being an old soldier, and discharged as unfit for service, with a recommendation to the board for a pension, where it seems nothing could be done, as no provision had been made for superannuated soldiers since the revolutionary war; which occasioned me to be destitute of support, except that which Providence threw in my way.

"Well, good man," said he, "you are a stranger to me; however, I will do all in my power for you, for God only knows what I may come to myself; my father is a seafaring man, and perhaps now may want assistance."

By this time I began to feel in better spirits, and asked the lad his name and where he lived.

"My name," answered he, "is William Downes; I am an apprentice to Mr. Edwards, the cooper, who lives in Water street; he is a charitable man, which induces me making bold to invite you to come and tarry in his shop until you can do better."

I thanked him and immediately repaired to my new lodgings, where my only dependence for support was from what this boy could procure for me from his master's table.

One day being observed by the housekeeper in taking some victuals from the table she inquired into the cause, and being informed, said she "was happy in having it in her power to alleviate the distress of a fellow creature, as far as the extent of her contracted finances would admit of."

She proved as good as her word by sending by my kind benefactor some of the best victuals her master's table afforded. Which was the occasion of my situation being made known to Mr. and Mrs. Edwards, from whose kind hospitality I received adequate sustenance until it pleased kind Providence to open a way for my future support.

My hopes were still sanguine, particularly on my meeting with general [Henry] Knox, who informed me that at the ensuing session he doubted not but the pension act would be amended, and then I would certainly be put on the list.

Colonel Harmar likewise informed me that he would use his utmost endeavors in forwarding my case.

Shortly after, I got acquainted with an old continental officer, who kept store at the corner of Third and Market streets. He gave me a letter to the speaker of the house of assembly, Thomas Mifflin, Esq., requesting him to raise a subscription among the members of the house for my present relief. On his reading the letter, he desired me to tarry in the state house until the business of the house was over.

When the business of the day was over Mr. Mifflin read the letter to the gentlemen, and was the first in acquiescing with the requisition, therein mentioned, being followed by Robert Morris and the rest of the members present. On the clerk's counting the money, it amounted to nine pounds thirteen shillings.

The speaker then ordered him to deliver it to me. My gratitude on receiving this liberal donation may be easier imagined than expressed. Suffice it to say that I felt as if thunder struck; however, recovering myself I walked into the statehouse yard, where meeting with a fellow, whom I believed to be a sharper, who accosted me saying, "Shaw, I can tell you where you can get well used for your money; and I will go with you, provided you treat me to a grog."

I answered him saying, "I could find people enough to take a shilling out of my pocket, but none to put a penny into it."

I started and never stopped until I got to my old friend Apkey's and paid him off my score, then repaired to a slop-shop where I equipped myself with a suit of clothes from head to foot.

The next day I left the city, and had not traveled over 15 or 16 miles before I was overtaken by two gentlemen, who asked me "if my name was not corporal John Robert Shaw, formerly under the command of colonel Harmar."

"Yes, please your honors, gentlemen, I belonged to captain McCurdy's company."

"Have you got the amount of a subscription from colonel Harmar?"

"No, I have got a subscription from the general assembly."

The gentlemen then observed that "colonel Harmar had collected 15 pounds when they left Philadelphia, and by then supposed that he must have increased it to 20 pounds."

They then enquired if I had any money.

I answered, yes, a little, upon which they gave me more money and desired me to go on to the next tavern; from whence they would write to colonel Harmar to send the money on by lieut. B.; then ordered the landlord to let me have what refreshment I wanted and they would pay for it.

In a few days lieut. B--- came. I went and spoke to him concerning the money, which he took amiss and threatened to horse whip me if I did not proceed on my journey.

My confidence in colonel Harmar was such that I then thought he had sent the money on by lieut. B.--, which B.

denied, though he promised me to write to colonel Harmar requesting of him to deposit the money with lawyer Clymer, a gentleman of Reading, a particular friend of mine.

I will hereafter have occasion to mention what became of this money.

Proceeding on my way to Lancaster, from thence to Carlisle, where I continued for some time in extreme distress, but was providentially relieved by a friend whom I met there, who, besides administering to my immediate necessities, wrote a petition for me, setting forth in a pathetic manner my misfortunes and inability to work; which petition was signed by the magistrates and the most respectable inhabitants of Carlisle.

From Carlisle I proceeded to Little York,[12] where I got the name of the gentleman beggar, particularly owing to my appearing as clean in my dress as my indigent circumstances would admit of. I always made it a point to be unassuming and civil, which was the cause of my being well treated wherever I came, one house excepted, which was that of an Englishman living in Pennsylvania.

At this man's house I called one frosty night, and asked for quarters. The man of the house invited me in, and told me to sit down by the stove, introducing me at the same time to his wife. When I got a little warm, a conversation took place in which I endeavored to entertain them with the occurrences of my past life, after which the man of the house took down his violin and played several tunes; when done his wife asked him into another room to supper, leaving poor pilgarlic ["poor me"] behind the stove both hungry and weary, having nothing to refresh myself with.

When they had done, he again repeated his music, and shortly after withdrew to bed, leaving me to pick out the softest plank for my bed and pillow; however, lying down hoping for better times I rested tolerably well, considering my hard fare.

The next morning the landlord accosted me very politely with, "Good morning to you, sir, how did you rest last night?"

I thanked him (for the compliment but not for the bed) and told him I rested very well.

I then proceeded on for Marsh Creek settlement, from thence to Hunterstown,[13] and so on to Gettys-town,[14] to Jockeytown[15] and then back to Little York; through York barrens to the Straw tavern, crossing the Susquehanna at Bald Friar ferry; proceeding to Nottingham township, thence through Chester county to Oxford,[16] and then to Octoraro,[17] where I stopped one night.

It being snowing and extremely cold, I went to the house of a Mr. Smith (a seceding minister) requesting liberty of him to lie that night by his kitchen fire. He answered he would not admit strangers into his house, but coming to the door and pointing towards a neighbouring house, observed that the man of that house entertained every distressed traveler that came that way.

So off I hobbled in the dark, in hopes of finding the house, but unfortunately missed the way by taking the wrong path, which brought me to a widow's house; where knocking at the door the old lady made her appearance, when I asked for quarters; she observed that being a poor widow and having no person about the house but herself and daughter, she was dubious of admitting strangers. Well, said I, if you will but let me warm myself, I flatter myself you will not turn me out this dismal cold night; accordingly she admitted me to her fire, where when I had warmed myself, I unbound my feet and shewed her the situation I was in from the frost; and likewise observed to her the treatment I had met with from Mr. Smith, which induced her to pity me, and to observe that I was welcome to whatever the house could afford and immediately provided me with a warm supper and a comfortable bed.

When I lay down, I ruminated considerable time on what kind Providence had done for me, in sending me to this poor widow's house. The pleasing thought occasioned me to feel at that time as happy as Mr. Smith with all his riches.

Next morning the widow's daughter went to Mr. Culbertson's (a covenanter minister). This was the man to whom Smith directed me the preceding evening. She told him in what manner Smith had treated me.

On the girl's return home, she brought me an invitation from Mr. Culbertson and his lady, requesting me to go to their house, which I gladly embraced after taking leave of my hospitable hostess and daughter.

On my arrival at Mr. Culbertson's, I was kindly invited in; and after a short conversation, was requested to tarry as long as I thought proper. The next day Mrs. Culbertson and her daughter (named Sally) cut me out some shirts and made them; the rest of my clothes they had washed and mended for me.

Here was a heaven on earth to me whilst I stayed, which was twelve days.—Not willing to encroach any longer on his kind hospitality, particularly as I observed him to be daily troubled with distressed travelers. On my departure Mr. Culbertson and family gave me a pressing invitation to call on them if ever I traveled that way, and that I would meet with the same hospitable reception.

Starting from Mr. Culbertson's I proceeded to Charlestown in Maryland, and there, meeting with a person who demanded of me a pass, I observed that I thought my disabled situation was pass sufficient; which satisfied him.

So proceeding on to Robert Lastley's near North East bay, where I continued until my feet got better and my strength recruited, doing small jobs occasionally about the house; but some misunderstanding taking place, I left there and proceeded to Jacob McDill's in Pickway, where I undertook a large job of ditching, which, when nearly completed, I was recommended by said McDill to a Robert Biers, with whom I engaged to dig 170 rod of large and small ditches which I soon accomplished.

Soon after, I started down for Chester county, and commenced working for one Francis Hoops, a Quaker. I made no bargain with the man, any further than that he told me he would reward me according to my merit; accordingly to work I went and can solemnly declare that daylight never caught me in bed during that winter which I worked for him, besides doing everything in my power to render satisfaction to the family; particularly to the woman part, which as a point I made never to deviate from.

But alas! I found it all in vain, and therefore on the first of March I demanded a settlement, in hopes of getting something for my labor. How unspeakable was my surprise when Hoops said, "John, thee may think thyself well paid."

Said I, "You know, Francis, that I received only 33 shillings for my three months' work. If this be ample reward for my labor in this world, I hope God will reward you in the next according to your deeds here; for 'cursed is he who defraudeth a labourer of his hire.'"

I complained to the elders of the meeting, but being poor and Hoops rich, consequently received no redress.

I leave you to judge, reader, what sort of a conscience (or whether any) this meek and lowly Quaker must possess. However, I soon engaged with a man of the name of Barrack Mitchener (a neighbor of Hoops) for six dollars per month, to quarry stone and burn lime, with whom I lived six months; and then hired with Thomas Butler of London-grove township[18] to quarry stone, where I had the misfortune of breaking my leg, which was occasioned as follows:

After blasting some rocks, I went to wedging some more, when the sledge glanced against the wedge which struck me on the leg. I dropped for dead, and lay there for some time, no one being convenient to assist me. After recovering a little, I crawled on my hands and knees, a half mile through forest and snow, which made my situation almost desperate.

The kind invitation of my friendly host Culbertson now occurred to me, to whose neighborhood I was conveyed next day on horseback.

I took up my quarters at the house of Daniel McCready, where I had the attendance of doctor Culbertson (the son of my benefactor) under whose care I continued about eight weeks and then returned to my former occupation of stone quarrying.

I now began to be weary of a single life (being two years a widower) therefore paid my addresses to a young Irish girl, by means of which I learned a new mode of courting, which is generally styled bundling.

The mode pursued is, after the old people retired, my Dulcinea took me by the hand and led me to her bed chamber (where a hint being as good as a nod for a blind horse) to bed we went and spent the night very agreeably. This mode of courtship, I understand, is fashionable in different parts of the union, and I flatter myself not disagreeable to the young folks.

After living here some time I got into the diabolical habit of fortune-telling, in which calling there is a great deal of confederacy. In pursuing this honourable calling, I got the appellation of the English fortune-teller. Here I also got acquainted with a quack doctor, who told me he would undertake to make me take a distaste against spiritous liquor, for which I agreed to give him half a guinea.

He accordingly got two live eels and put them into a quart bottle, filled with rum, letting them stand for three or four days; then gave me a portion every third day, until I began to grow weary of the medicine; having every reason to believe it would not answer the desired effect, consequently declined taking any more of it.

Shortly I heard of a Doctor Murray in Lancaster, whom I

had every reason to believe could perform the much wished for cure. I accordingly made application to him, who agreed to cure me for three half joes.

He therefore prepared a potion, part of which I was to take every two days until the cure was effected; however, I had not taken it long before I began to swell and froth at the mouth like a madman. True it is it had like to have proved an effectual cure by sending me to the other world.

Soon after this a Mrs. McHarrey offered to cure me of this dreadful propensity; to which I agreed, and she accordingly administered a dose to me, sufficient to have killed a horse; the result of which was my being in five minutes time sicker than ever I remembered to have been with the bottle fever in my life. By this time I found out that nothing but fortitude and a good resolution could be an antidote against drinking ardent liquors to an excess.

Chapter 8

"I got the name of a water witch."

Shortly after, I took a tour to New London, through Chester county to Newark; from thence to Christein bridge, where I commenced work with one Joseph Hogle. Continuing here but a short time, I started again for Philadelphia to Wilmington, and so on to Chester, where stopping at a tavern I refreshed myself.

I had not been long there before a young woman came in; I invited her to drink, after which a conversation took place, in which she informed me she intended traveling beyond Darby, but should tarry there for her brother. So I bid her farewell and pursued my journey; but did not proceed far until I stopped at a man's door and fell into a conversation with him. We had not long conversed before the young woman above mentioned passed me.

I soon followed and came up with her, accosting her with, well overtaken, young woman. She observed she would be glad of my company, as there was no probability of her brother coming up.

"Thank you, madam, if my company be agreeable we will travel together as far as you go by my road."

So on we jogged, as happy as king and queen. I learned from her conversation that she had an uncle living about two miles from Darby, to whose house she gave me an invitation to go with her; with which I cheerfully complied.

Night coming on, and growing weary, we sat down to rest, when an innocent conversation took place, to the following purport:

"My dear, I should think myself the happiest man on earth, if allowed to kiss your sweet lips."

This request she kindly complied with, after which some natural familiarities took place between us (which may better be imaged than expressed) that induced her to throw her arms around me, saying, "My dear, will you not marry me?"

"Yes, my love, certainly, we shall get married tomorrow."

So on we jogged to her uncle's, who, with his family, was in bed. So I proposed lodging in the barn, to which my intended bride agreed; in we went, made ourselves a bed of hay, on which we agreeably spent the night.

In the morning I went out, and made my escape with all possible haste across the country, leaving my disappointed bride expecting every moment (I suppose) my return, in order to perform my promise of marriage, which to this day I have neglected fulfilling with her.

I crossed the country to Dickworthstown,[1] where I lodged that night, and drinking some hard cider which occasioned me to be taken short in the night, unfortunately there was no chamberpot in the room, nor yet could I get the window or door open, which occasioned me to have recourse to my hat, which I well filled before morning.

Rising at daylight, and going downstairs, with my new constructed conveniency under my arm, was called to by the hostler, saying, "Who comes there?"

"A friend," said I.

"I doubt it," said he. "What's that you have under your arm?"

"Come and see," said I.

Accordingly he came, and going to lay hold of the hat, I caught his hand and put it into the hat, which made him bestow a volley of abuse on me.

I started on to the Sign of the Red Eagle, sixteen miles and a half from Philadelphia, kept by Adam Cryder, with whom I hired as an hostler, but soon grew weary of that business.

I therefore determined to try my fortune once more in Philadelphia. On my arrival there (being in the evening) I repaired to Newmarket, where being invited to a frolic, was introduced to a fine parcel of ladies (all mother Carey's chickens). I had not been long there before I made choice of one of them to spend the night with, and called for a room, where we had not been long before we were disturbed by one of the men from a back room, much intoxicated and as destitute of clothes as when born, which disgusted me so much that I withdrew and left my fair one to sleep without my company that night.

My name being established in the country as a well digger, I was accordingly sent for by a certain Joe Wilson, living on the Lancaster road, 15 miles from Philadelphia, with whom I commenced digging a well, which went 16 feet into a solid rock. After the completion of which I opened an old well, which had been left unfinished for 52 years; at which I made very rapid progress, and soon insured to finish it for him, even provided the devil was at the bottom of it; which I accordingly did, though unfortunately it had like to have cost me dear.

For unthinkingly leaving a loose rock in the side of the

well, 27 feet from the bottom, and thinking I had got a sufficient depth under water, I called Mr. Wilson to come down into
the well and satisfy himself; he had not been there 15 minutes
before accidentally looking up, he cried out, "Shaw, the well is
caving in."

I looked up and to my great surprise saw the rock above
mentioned, tumbling down, which struck the bottom of the
well first, then rolled on my left leg, then on Wilson's left arm,
which it broke in pieces, and there held us fast until the
neighbors extricated us.

This I look upon as one of the most providential escapes of
my life, particularly when I inform you, reader, that it took two
blasts before it could be got out. My leg was not much injured,
but Mr. Wilson will remain a cripple the residue of his days.

After finishing the well, I felt anxious for a frolic, and
therefore started for Philadelphia (where I paid for the roast
before I got back) arriving at the Sign of the White Horse,[2] was
there ordered to assist in conveying a madman to bedlam.

On our way we stopped at the Sign of the Unicorn for
refreshment, where I beheld a ghastly sight, a poor unfortunate
man who the day before fell into the fire in a pit and burnt his
eyes out, and his head to a cinder. The sight of these two
unfortunate objects made such an impression on me that I could
not rest for several nights after. I thought I saw the madman
grinning me in the face and the unfortunate dead man following
me with his ghastly appearance.

We soon arrived in the city, where I left my company and
went to one of my old rendezvous, at the Sign of the Three Jolly
Irishmen, in Water street; here I began my career.

Getting in company with a blade, equally as anxious for
frolicking as myself, we began with a gallon of mulled beer,
qualified with a quart of good spirits, in the punishing of which
we were joined by some interlopers and half a dozen fine girls
with a piper and fiddler.

These composed our jolly group, where we spent the day merrily; and late at night broke up, pretty well done over. However, being determined to enjoy the pleasures of the night as well as the day, I proceeded with my doxy to her lodgings. Being introduced to the landlady, was invited upstairs into a room, with a good bed and otherwise equipped for entering on the wars of Venus.

But alas! How disappointed were my hopes; for when stripped and ready to jump into the arms of my fair one, I unfortunately (at her request) stepped to put the candle out, when lo! the floor gradually sunk, and in a few seconds I found myself landed in a back street, with no other covering to guard me against the inclemency of a cold winter night than my shirt. Finding myself completely done over, I repaired to my old quarters, where the landlord gave me some old clothes to cover my nakedness.

I put on a bold face to try my fortune once more, and left the city, it being the middle of winter, without shoes or stockings, the rest of my clothes not being worth one dollar, the ground slightly frozen over not sufficient to bear me up, consequently occasioned the blood to flow abundantly over my feet.

On the evening of that day which I left the city I called for quarters at a tavern, where I spent freely going down.

The landlord looking at me, observed, he was afraid I would rob his house. I must confess that my appearance was by no means prepossessing; however, he invited me to the fire where I tarried all night, when next morning he asked how he would dispose of me in case I died.

I told him to dig a hole and bury me in it, which he was not at the trouble of doing, but sent me along with some wagoners, amongst whom was a jolly young man that had drunk a little of the same bitter cup amongst the ladies in Philadelphia.

He said he would assist me, and accordingly did, by tipping me a little out of brown Bet, which contained some double fortified stimulous.

Parting with the wagoners, I trudged on till I came within a mile of the White Horse where, meeting with three old soldiers, one of whom formerly belonged to captain McCurdy's company, in the first American regiment, commanded by that undaunted hero, colonel Josiah Harmar, whose name ought to be written in letters of gold.

The old soldier gave me a pair of shoes, and recommended me to stop at the White Horse whose landlord was particularly charitable to old soldiers. I took his advice and shortly arrived there.

There being a foxhunt in the neighborhood that day, occasioned the house to be thronged; however, they made way for me to the fire, where I experienced great pain. However, the landlord gave me every assistance in his power and sent me on in a wagon to Downingtown, across Brandywine to the Sign of the Ship.

There I took off the main road and made inquiry for colonel Humpton, formerly commander of the sixth Pennsylvania regiment, who treated me with genuine hospitality—supplying me with a complete suit of clothes, some money and a pair of crutches, with which I jogged on to a tavern where I took up my quarters.

There happened to be a Mr. John Boyd and a Mr. Printer in the house, who lived in Octoraro and to whose bounty I am much indebted. I tarried there until I got well, where leaving my crutches, I pushed for Chester county, to my old friends, the Quakers, where word was left for me that a certain Abraham Gibbons, a Quaker preacher from near Lancaster, had a well to finish that six other diggers had given up.

I undertook to finish the well or lose my labor. My employer being a droll old fellow, I cannot help mentioning a joke that happened between him and a curious old Irishman: A conversation took place one day at dinner on faith, when the Quaker observed that he had faith enough to walk on water without sinking; so their going to work, they had to cross a creek, over which lay a log, the Irishman being behind as the Quaker was crossing, gave the log a shake, when down drops poor broad-brim, up to his neck in the water.

"Ah, dear Abraham," said Pat, "where is thy faith now?"

"Friend," said Abraham, "thou hast outwitted me."

I shortly finished the well, for which I was honourably paid.

I then went to dig a well for a Mr. Miller near New Holland, and setting one Sunday evening near the door in company with the said Miller and family, we heard the report of a gun not far distant; however, taking no notice of it but retired to bed, from which we shortly were disturbed by some of the neighbors coming in, ordering us to meet at a certain mill, which we did.

Immediately after, two young men having passed that way, and stopping at a house, gave a young woman one dollar for washing some blood off their shirt sleeves; being asked what occasioned it, said they had almost killed old McCastleton, and were going to a Mr. M.--- where they could be found if necessary.

Shortly after, a man came along and found the old man dead in a wagon rut, which gave the alarm to the neighbourhood, and occasioned about 60 of us to meet at the aforesaid mill, where dividing in different parties, it fell to my lot to be of the party that took the culprits.

We bound them and brought them to where the dead man lay, but they denied the fact. However, we conveyed them to Lancaster, where we arrived about sunrise and took them before Squire Hubley, who committed them to prison. I was surprised to see the levity of one of them, a lad not exceeding 14, who seemed to make little of his situation, which appeared as if he could foretell what the event would be; for when they were tried, they were acquitted for want of evidence.

I began to grow weary of that part of the country, so pushed on to Lancaster, determined on a frolic; putting up at Adamstown,[3] I soon met with plenty of boon companions to help in carrying on the caper.

Here I gave myself the name of Peter Alexander Wild-Goose, and generally went by the name of Wild-Goose the madman. The young bucks of the town frequently making me groggy, for which I gave them Morgan Rattler in style.

One day going to see the curiosities of Mr. Whitman's brewery, he and some more gentlemen happened to be there, when the conversation turned on the size of the kettles. He observed that one of them contained 500 gallons. I swore he was a liar, for which he said I should give him gentlemanly satisfaction; accordingly I started off for my sword, but totally forgot ever to return.

Off I started to the country, resolved to take up my old trade of basket weaving; however, at this time I engaged with a Mr. Holes, to work at the mine banks, in company with an old soldier, who loved a drop of a dram as well as myself.

Here I had the pleasure of getting acquainted with a widow, whose acquaintance seemed very agreeable. One evening, being in company with her over a bottle of good whiskey, the conversation turned on matrimony, which I evaded, and it growing late, proposed going to bed, which my buxom widow agreed to; where we spent a most agreeable night, with a promise of my repeating it.

But next morning I left both the mine bank and the widow, and proceeded on to within 10 miles of Lancaster, where I engaged to quarry 1,000 perch of stone for John Shank, whom I found to be an ill-disposed person. He having 30 men at work for him in building a grist mill, with every man of whom (when the first story was built) he fell out.

Off then I started for New Holland, where I undertook to dig a quantity of wells. The names of the people for whom I dug and the depth of the wells as follows:

Adam Miller	17 feet	
William Clark	23 feet, chiefly rock	
John Hance	10 and quarried 30 perch stone	
Thomas Taylor	19	
Alexander Mahoney	30	
George Aire	14, burnt 3360 bus. of lime.	
John Painter	16	
Thomas Harris	52	
Robert Hamilton	36	
John Peters	24	dug 300 yards of ditching
William Reynolds	14	
Andrew Numan	23	
Gaspar Yordan	23	40 rods of mill race & 4 cellars
John Rhodes	26	6 cellars
John Wilson	57	
William Kasill	16	
Job Pyle	14	
Abraham Penick	40	
Joseph Preston	24	
Thomas Morton	20	
Abraham Gibbons	14	
William Pugee	19	
John Hamilton	9	

Total, 589 all in Pennsylvania[4]

In 1791 I was sent for to Lebanon to hunt water, where I got the name of a water witch. During my continuance there, a company of six months men, commanded by captain Payette halted here being on their way for the western country. I went to see if there were any of my old comrades amongst them, (being fond of the company of an old soldier) and found two, with whom I spent a jovial night, and the next morning making too free with my bitters, the general beat, which elevated me so that I fell in and marched all day, and halting in the evening, I began to cut some didos, bantering the captain or his men to go through the manual exercise, which occasioned the captain taking more notice of me, and proposed enlisting me, (he not knowing my decripped state) accordingly, I enlisted and we marched on for Carlisle and encamped on the commons.

A quarter guard being called out, it fell to my lot to be on duty, and placed as sentry over the captain's marquee, was challenged by a gentleman (an aquaintance of the captain's) inquiring if my name was not John Robert Shaw.

I answered yes, but requested no discourse of him whilst on sentry, which he politely declined. However, after I came off duty, my captain sent for me and told me that Mr. Creathe (merchant in Carlisle) requested me to call on him, which I accordingly did; and never in my life was more hospitably treated than I was by himself, his family, and captain Alexander, his son-in-law, to whose benevolent hospitality I shall during my existence ever remain grateful.

We marched on through the different towns until we arrived at Pittsburgh, where we continued until the arrival of the rest of the army from the different states, then embarking in 23 different boats for Fort Washington.[5]

It fell to my lot to go in a boat belonging to a Mr. Holsted (a sutler) where I officiated as helmsman, in which I was very fortunate, never getting aground the whole voyage, though other boats were continually striking.

I remember going to shore and observing an uncommon large sycamore tree, had the curiosity to measure it and (almost incredible to tell) found it measured 25 feet in diameter.[6]

In 21 days from our embarkment we arrived at Fort Washington, and encamped and when rested the companies commenced drilling, which was a good opportunity for displaying my knowledge of tactics, which occasioned me to be appointed drill sergeant of the company, which I divided into grand and awkward squads; all the experienced soldiers I put into the grand squad and the unexperienced into the awkward; according to the progress of the latter they were admitted into the former.

Our general orders were to drill three times a day; but my squads wishing to excel took every opportunity of becoming acquainted with tactics; in which I was particular in facilitating their progress.

I pursued the plan instilled in me by old corporal Coggle, of the 33d regiment, whose knowledge in tactics was not excelled, perhaps by any soldier in the union.

I always acted as fugleman and commander in putting them through the manual exercises, after Steuben's improved plan, taking particular care to give them an erect and soldierly appearance, both in attitude, look and walk. After while I taught them to wheel and form in every position, from right to left, and from left to right, and from the center, until I had them sufficiently versed in all the evolutions.

After this procedure, I put a firelock into their hands and made them acquire a thorough command of it. Through my indefatigable assiduity and skill, I brought my squad so forward in a short time as to be considered as good disciplinarian as any in the garrison. As a proof for which I refer my reader to major David Zeigler (now residing in Cincinnati), lieutenant Whistler, and sergeant major Bennet, whose knowledge that way is inferior to none in the United States.

One day being walking in the garrison accompanied by an old soldier, of a sudden was accosted by general Harmar (who had just resigned his command to general St. Clair) asking me if my name was not Shaw.

I answered, "Yes, please, your honor."

"Did I not discharge you in 1785 as unfit for duty?"

"Yes, your honor."

Upon which he desired me to come into the room, where he represented my case to general St. Clair and the rest of the officers, giving them a correct account of my performance and unhappy disaster at Fort McIntosh, and said, "I was not fit for a soldier and ought to be discharged;" asking me how I became enlisted; the particulars of which I informed him of, and requested of him to speak to general St. Clair to allow me to perform garrison duty, as I thought myself as capable of performing such duty as any man in the army, which was readily granted.

I then took the liberty of asking colonel Harmar whether or not he received some money by subscription for me in Philadelphia and if not delivered into the hands of a Mr. ---

"Yes," replied he, "and did you never receive it?"

I answered no; then gave him an account of what I had received from the members of the legislature—my leaving the city—being met by two gentlemen—their kind treatment of me—my delaying three days on the road for Mr. --- his treatment to me, etc.

"Well," says the colonel, "Mr.--- will be down the river shortly, and I will make him give you the money."

He came, it is true, but he being of a sanguinary disposition and an officer induced me never to trouble him for it.

In the course of a few weeks the army received marching orders, and myself with every man unfit for actual service were ordered into the garrison under the command of lieut. Pasmore. Here I remained a few weeks, in the course of which the lieutenant received recruiting orders, at which time I was on the commissary's guard.

A sergeant came there with an order for me to go to the lieutenant, who gave me a bounty of six dollars, enlisting me for three years, unless sooner discharged.

I then requested of him to give me four days liberty to spend my bounty in, which he complied with. Accordingly away I went, got half a dozen canteens, repaired to town to one Kelley's, a piper, called for a good grog, got my canteens filled, and began to make merry, but did not enjoy myself long before I

was sent for by the lieutenant, who on my arrival informed me
the doctor would not pass, nor the muster master muster me.

So I told him I had spent part of the bounty in the purchase
of rum, which I hoped he would admit into the barracks, which
he accordingly did, allowing me one day to get drunk and
another to get sober, and making me a present of another dollar
besides that one I spent; this with many other favors I received
from lt. Pasmore, particularly that of his allowing me to work in
the town, where I dug the first well that ever was in Cincinnati,[7]
and by my directions the well in the garrison was finished,
besides a number of other wells which I laid off, and which have
been finished since my leaving there, which is a clear demon-
stration of the infallibility of the forked rod.

For I do maintain that there is no danger of failing in
procuring water, provided a man digs to the depth prescribed by
the man who carries the rod and understands the efficacy of it.

In the course of some time, I was one of a command, who
went to drive cattle to the army. We drove on to Fort Hamilton[8]
and across the Great Miami, and at night took up our quarters
on good camping ground, where we baked up all our flour, little
thinking how much need some of our fellow soldiers stood in for
food.

However, next morning proved to us the certainty of it, for
by 11 o'clock we were met by five of the cavalry, who communicated to us the news of general St. Clair's defeat and which
communication they were carrying to Fort Hamilton.

The news had a disagreeable effect on some of our party,
who were immediately seized with cannon fever, and retreated
with all possible expedition back to Fort Hamilton, where they
received the punishment due for desertion and cowardice.

However, the rest of us (six out of eleven) proceeded on
with our cattle and shortly met the retreating army, (a sight truly
grating to us) some wounded and the whole of them starving
and dejected. To work they went, and in a few minutes slayed

half a dozen of our bullocks, stewing them up in a quick time, without paying any particular attention to the nicety of the cooking.

However, we left them enjoying themselves in their luxury and proceeded on to Fort Jefferson,[9] where the sight of our cattle was a pleasing object, particularly as they had been subsisting on horse flesh for some days prior to our arrival.

The next morning we started back to Fort Hamilton and from there to Fort Washington; and when we arrived there we encamped in a very disagreeable situation, and suffered extremely from the inclemency of the weather.

In a short time we were all discharged without any prospect of being paid, however, myself and two more sold our certificates for a mere trifle and crossed the Ohio for Kentucky, and proceeded on till we came to Campbell's station,[10] where we stopped all night, one of my comrades selling a pair of stockings to pay for our supper, being all the provisions we received until we arrived in Georgetown.

But before we arrived there we took up our night's lodging near Elkhorn, in Craig's sawmill house,[11] in as cold, hungry, and naked and in fact miserable and lousy a situation as ever I remember to have been in.

Next morning we proceeded to town, and stopping at the house of a Mr. McQuiddy, requesting of him liberty to warm ourselves, which he complied with. While there I observed an oven full of Irish potatoes and roast beef, which smelled so sweet that I longed to be tugging at them.

After a little conversation we requested to tarry all night, to which the landlord did not seem to consent, but observed that there was an old schoolhouse not far off where we might stay.

The hopes of enjoying some of the beef and potatoes, together with the pleasing appearance of the landlady, I by no means wished to change for the uncomfortable lodging in a cold and dreary schoolhouse. However, by the intercession of the landlady we were allowed to stay all night and likewise partook of the beef and potatoes.

Next morning, observing a pile of wood, we cut it up by way of compensation for our supper and lodging.

By this time we began to deliberate what we should follow in this strange country for a living. One of our company quitting us, (the other being a New Jersey man).

I heard of a certain Mr. Laughead, living about six miles from Lexington. We started for there. On coming to the house, knocked and asked liberty to warm ourselves, which was readily granted; shortly after made application to stay all night. The landlady hesitated a little, saying her husband was not at home, but by her brother's interceding for us, she gave up. Her brother was acquainted with the hardships attending war, being formerly embarked in it, and now a militia captain. He gave us a great deal of encouragement concerning this country, and an invitation to stay in the neighborhood telling us there were two of his tenants who wanted men to hire.

Here we dropped the conversation for that night, it being far spent, and being invited to supper, induced me to suppose myself amongst my old Pennsylvania farmers.

I now began to enquire of the woman of the house what her husband's name was, and being informed it was Laughead, then asked if he was related to a man of that name in Octoraro, (observing her color change) she answered yes, that is my husband's father, do you know him?

I answered I did and his daughter Jenny; that I formerly lived with a Mr. Culbertson, a covenanting minister, and that Mr. Laughead was one of his elders, which occasioned me to be well acquainted with him.

By this time the landlady seemed very well pleased, asking me many questions about the covenanters and seceders in Pennsylvania, until bedtime came on, when she proposed making us a bed on the floor; but we honestly opposed it, telling her that we were lousy and not fit to sleep in a bed.

She in a few minutes brought me a clean shirt, which made my comrade uneasy, observing, "Shaw, how come this, that you are so much more in favor than I?"

"Because," said I, "you look like a Jersey-Blue and I like a Pennsylvania farmer."

But I had scarce uttered these words when she brought him another, which occasioned him to laugh with both sides of his mouth. She likewise brought us some old clothes to lie on, and then retired for the night.

After which we stripped ourselves and committed our old shirts to the flames, from whence we heard the cracking of the gentry very plain. Then putting on our clean linen, we lay down and slept exceedingly well.

Early the next morning captain Mitchell (her brother) returned with some clothing which he generously distributed between us, and directed us to his tenants, as observed before.

It fell my lot to engage with a Mr. Lanterman, with whom I bargained to maul 540 rails for a new shirt (it being a business I had never been used to) however by the dint of hard labor, I soon earned my shirt.

My comrade engaged with a Mr. Applegate to break flax, but being of a bad disposition, he soon fell out with his landlady, consequently left there and likewise enticed me away from Mr. Lanterman's.

Chapter 9

"She married and left me as usual like the done-over tailor."

y comrade and I started on our road to Frankfort, calling at general Wilkinson's,[1] who politely treated us to a grog and advised us to go to the salt works; he likewise generously put us across the river.

After we crossed the river the first house we stopped at proved to be a particular acquaintance of mine from Pittsburgh (Mr. Haymaker), who treated us with kind hospitality, advising us not to go to the salt works; for, said he, "It is a hell on earth."

From his house we started in the morning with grateful hearts for Arnold's station,[2] (making inquiry on the road for Jersey and Pennsylvania people). When we arrived at captain Arnold's house, he generously invited us to dinner, which was truly acceptable.

My comrade inquired if there were any Jersey people convenient to there. Captain Arnold observed his father came from Jersey, and he made no doubt that he would give him work; upon which we started on to Baker's tavern, where we had not been long before some men came to the house, amongst whom were old Mr. Arnold, and with whom my comrade soon made a bargain to work, and trudged off, leaving poor old Shaw to shift as well as he could.

I proceeded to Mr. McGuire's, who lived in the vicinity, and asked for quarters, which was granted.

Soon after my arrival my landlord inquired which way I was traveling. I told him I could not tell how far, but that I was in pursuit of work, which I was willing to do for my victuals and whatever other compensation my employer thought proper. He told me I need go no further, asking me what I could do; to which I answered a number of domestic affairs, such as to wait on his lady, etc.

The following morning after breakfast my employer walked to a new improvement (a handsome situation) where he had built a double log house after the Virginia fashion (without a cellar). I asked the cause of his so doing, he observed that the foundation was a solid rock, and that the cellar would cost him more than the house.

I told him provided he furnished me with some powder and the necessary tools, that I would blow him out a cellar, for a shirt and a pair of shoes; to which he agreed, and accordingly furnished me with a set of new fashioned tools indeed. Suffice it to say that by the dint of assiduity and elbow grease, I soon earned my shirt and shoes, and that much to the satisfaction of my employer; after which I built him a lime kiln.

Mr. McGuire, observing a number of his hogs to be badly torn, naturally conjectured it must have been done by a panther, therefore proposed a hunting frolic to me, to which I readily agreed.

We started and had not traveled far before we came on the track of two panthers; proceeding on about a quarter of a mile, I observed one of them on the limb of a large tree; calling out to McGuire (and being entirely unacquainted with the different quadrupeds) yonder is a deer on the limb of that tree, which deer or rather panther, he observing, immediately fired and wounded it, after which it jumped down and pursued different directions, receiving three different wounds before we killed it; and out of his skin I made myself a good pair of shoes.

On the first day of March (1792) I started from Mr. McGuire's, who satisfied me well for my winter's work, pursuing my way across Steel's ferry, and along the north side of the Kentucky river, until I came to Joseph McLain's, where I blew some rocks for him.

After which I proceeded to one Abraham Morten's (Jessamine)[3] with whom I agreed to split 5,000 rails. Here was the first place I understood that cutting and splitting one hundred rails per day was not thought a day's work for a man, being the second time I undertook such a job. I first began with 40, but soon found that I could easily accomplish 200, and could do were I acquainted with the different sorts of timber, a fourth more in a day.

I then commenced with a certain capt. — to blow rocks and quarry stone, and after working with him a considerable time, he insidiously endeavored to defraud me out of my hire; and with a great deal of persuasion prevailed with him to pay me half of it, considering half a loaf better than no bread.

After receiving my half stipend, I proceeded to the mouth of Hickman,[4] where I got pretty well fuddled, and went to the boat intending to cross, but Mr. Ballenger, the ferryman, observing my intoxication, would not admit me into the boat, consequently returned to the ferry house (Mr. Scott's)[5] where I spent the remainder of my hard-earned money; the result of which was a violent attack of the bottle fever, but the commisseration, assiduity and kind attention of Mr. and Mrs. Scott to me at that time shall always be impressed on my heart, therefrom never to be erased.

After recovering from my indisposition I commenced digging a well for John Biswell, four miles from Mr. Scott's ferry; a storm coming on prevented me from progressing; therefore turned to my old trade of frolicing, the result as usual—the bottle fever.

Afflicted with it, I was one night lying in the tavern before the fire, when I was disturbed by a parcel of ruffians, consisting of major Mastin Clay, lieutenant Spence, a Mr. Moss and Sow. They entered the house and had not been there long before making inquiry of the landlord who I was.

He answered, "Old Shaw the well digger, who is very sick."

"Damn him," observed Clay, "let us have a little fun with him."

With that he laid a chunk of fire on my leg, which burnt me severely.

I jumped on my feet requesting of them to let me alone, saying I was then sick and no person to take my part, but even so, I would try the best of them singly; this exasperated them, and Clay being the greatest scoundrel among them, urged the rest to lay hold of me, which they did, compelling a negro who was in the house to butt me with his head and gouge me severely.

I observed to Clay that if ever an opportunity offered I should pay him off in equal coin, which I fortunately did. For shortly after, meeting him at Taylor's tavern in Lexington, I demanded satisfaction for the brutal treatment I had received from him; however, by the intercession of some friends, and his making ample concessions, we compromised the matter amicably.

I started from Jessamine (county) in the spring of 1793, and proceeded on to Clear creek, where I worked for Mr. Ephraim, James January, Joseph Wood, James Dunn, and William and Joseph Hughes, by all of whom I was well treated.

Leaving Clear creek, I went to Lexington where I engaged with one Trainer (a sort of tavern keeper) to quarry stone for him at two shillings per day—low wages but he still wanted me for less, and strove by every means in his power to take advantage of me.

His foreman, one Johnson, informed me that three blasts a day, from 10 to 12 inches deep was a good day's work for a man. I observed to him that such a man was not fit to work in a quarry, and bet him a wager of a bottle of whiskey that I could blow three blasts before breakfast, which I won. After which Mr. Trainer offered me a share in the quarry, which I refused, observing at the same time that I had not seen a man in Kentucky that I would join in that line of business with.

Shortly after, I commenced digging a well for one Samuel Lamb on Clear creek, who generously supplied me with money to buy tools; he likewise furnished me with a horse to ride to Lexington in order to purchase them, which I did, and on my return fell off the horse and had a very narrow escape for my life. The well I finished for Mr. Lamb, for which I was honorably paid.

It was about this time that I dreamed a singular dream, which was that I thought I heard a voice calling to me saying, "Shaw! Shaw! Repent or you will be damned." And in the course of a few weeks after, I dreamed another, in which I thought I heard the same voice saying, "Shaw! Shaw! Repent and you will be saved."

This last dream alarmed me so much that I awoke the family and communicated my dream to them.

There was in the house at that time a certain Andrew Ward, supposed to be a pious man, who exhorted me seriously to reform from the mode of life which I was in the habit of pursuing, and pointed out to me what must be the inevitable result of my perseverance therein, which I took extremely kind.

Leaving Mr. Lamb's, I came to Black's station;[6] and so on to Lexington, where I again commenced my mad career; falling in company with one Prothroe, who assiduously assisted in distributing my money.

My money being expended and having no place to stay, I requested liberty of this Prothroe to lie in a corner of his shop (he being a cabinet maker) until I got better (being at the time of course afflicted with my old complaint the bottle fever).

This he refused, observing I had no money, and therefore wished to have nothing to do with me, but immediately observing that if I would sign my name to a piece of blank paper, he would give me a dram; thinking no harm, I accordingly did, after which he insisted on my leaving the house, which I did in a very distressed situation, and went out to Maxwell's spring.[7]

There I drank a quantity of water, which occasioned me to vomit a quantity of blood.

Night coming on I walked along intending to take up my quarters in a friend's house, but growing weary and sick, I lay down in the woods, and shortly fell asleep, continuing so until midnight, when being awakened by a noise which I could not account for, I jumped up rather amazed, and within nine or ten feet of me saw a ball of fire, apparently as large as a bushel, and at the same time heard a voice over my head crying, "Shaw! Shaw! Will you not speak to me?"

A thousand conjectures now began to float in my head; I began to reflect on my former dreams—I rose and began to pray fervently, in which posture I did not long continue before those gloomy visions totally vanished.

I then proceeded further into the woods, but did not continue long there before I heard the voice and saw the fire as plain as before; however, day appearing, I felt relieved, and proceeded on the road, where I had not long continued before I observed a man walking alongside of me. On a close view of him, I found it to be the exact likeness of Prothroe, imagining in myself that he was killed, and that this my companion must be his ghost.

I then observed to him that I never did him any harm, therefore requested of him in God's name to leave me; at the name of God he immediately disappeared, and I continued on my journey, hoping the worst was over; but shocking to relate, I did not go far before he met me full in the face, in quite a different dress, when again using my former argument he again disappeared, and I proceeded to the five-mile cabin, where lo! again appeared my visitant dressed in black.

Being determined to ascertain whether or not it was substance, I made a grasp at him, and wonderful to relate! It vanished like an airy vision, but again appeared behind some logs, which lay convenient, beckoning me to come to him; I did and followed him from log to log until he vanished and left me extremely exhausted.

I then proceeded to the five-mile cabin, got the man of the house to accompany me part of the road towards Lexington, passing by a house, the woman gave me some breakfast, after which observing some drovers going by, with whom I traveled on to Lexington, my visiting ghost appearing to me in different shapes, forms, attitudes and dress, still beckoning me to approach him, which I now dreaded as he frequently appeared besmeared with blood; however, I found the name of God was my only safeguard, which I continually kept repeating to him, and he as continually disappearing until I arrived in Lexington.

When I arrived in Lexington, I immediately went to the house of Prothroe, and told him what I had seen, exhorting him to reform and strive to live a better life, observing to him that I feared something extraordinary would shortly happen from the omens that were portending.

He answered saying, "I am determined to live a more regular and Christian life, for indeed I had shocking dreams lately, which induce me to take up the resolution of becoming a better man."

I left the house and proceeded up the hill, and meeting

with Mr. Patterson and Ellison, who earnestly entreated me to quit the company of Prothroe, and to endeavor to lead a better and more uniform life.

Mr. Ellison politely invited me to his house, it being in the evening. After prayers, Mrs. Ellison made a pallet bed for me, where I had not long lain before I was astonished with the sight of the ball of fire and the voice calling me, "Shaw, won't you speak to me?"

I jumped on my feet calling to Mr. Ellison requesting of him for God's sake to go to prayer.

He immediately took a religious book and began reading. I seated myself alongside of him, with my head between my knees, when I thought I observed the hand of a man stretched towards me.

I then got up requesting him to let me read—he accordingly gave me the book, and rising up in order to bring another candle out of the next room, when I thought I observed a venerable old man standing between me and the door, with his gray locks hanging over his ears.

Mr. Ellison returned and remained with me some time, whilst I read. But growing sleepy, he called up two of his apprentices and then retired to bed. I continued reading until between the hours of 12 and 1, in company with the boys, when I imagined that I beheld rising at the end of the table, a head like a man's and eyes like two balls of fire, glaring me full in the face.

My astonishment at the horrid sight can be better imagined than expressed. However, I summoned fortitude enough to say, begone, Satan, or I'll shoot you with the Word of God; when immediately it disappeared, leaving behind a smoke similar to that which is produced by sulphur, which induced me to think it was the devil, and consequently no hopes for me.

My lost state appeared so apparent to me that I requested of Mr. Ellison to summon all the profligate youth and old drunkards in the town, in order to take warning by me and to avoid if possible the life I had pursued, and which brought me to this truly distressing situation. It being an unseasonable hour, Mr. Ellison declined calling them.

I continued in extreme distress, the devil (as I supposed) appearing to me in various forms too horrid to mention, until at length day appeared, to my inexpressible pleasure, which relieved me in part from my fancy-raised vision.

I requested Mr. Ellison to call in some pious men in order that I might converse and advise with them, amongst whom was a Mr. Adams (a Scotchman and a good one) who strenuously advised me to study the scriptures and to abide invariably to the precepts therein laid down. During the day my disturbed imagination still continued to raise up ideal apparitions, but at night when bedtime came on, I implored fervently the aid of that Supreme Being, who is the defender and support of all us miserable mortals, from which I felt relieved.

I tied a handkerchief around my eyes, went to bed and enjoyed as comfortable a night's rest as ever I experienced, after which I enjoyed a calm serenity, for the describing of which words are here denied me, and for which, my kind and candid readers, will I hope excuse me. Suffice it to say that I turned in to work for Mr. Ellison and made him a compensation for the trouble he had been at with me.

After compensating Mr. Ellison with my labor, for his trouble with me, Mr. James Parker asked me to finish a well that had been begun by Trainer, who refused giving it up, but Mr. Parker told him that he would not employ him any longer, as he considered him a troublesome, inattentive man, upon which Trainer gave up the well.

Accordingly I commenced digging at a dollar per day. I had not worked long at this well when I was visited by Prothroe, requesting me to fulfill the contents of an indenture which he said he held against me. I will here beg leave to trespass a little on my reader's patience, in order to be particular in developing fully the character of this nefarious swindler.

The reader must recollect reading in one of the preceding pages of my signing a blank paper at the request of Prothroe, which blank he filled up with an indenture binding me as a servant to him for three months, witnessed by some of his comrades of equal "honesty" with himself.

On his producing this indenture I was astonished, and thinking there was no alternative quitted my well and commenced working for him. However, taking into consideration that he acquired this instrument of writing unlawfully, I consulted some of my friends, who advised me to compromise the matter with him, which I did after paying him four pounds ten shillings in merchandise.

And now I call that Being to witness, who is and will be the eventual judge of all things, that I never directly nor indirectly owed this Prothroe one cent in my life.

I then returned to Mr. Parker's, where I had not worked long before I got ready for a blast, when throwing down the fire twice, and the shot not going off, I went down to prime afresh, but was not careful in scraping the coals away, and leaving some tow round the touch hole, which occasioned the priming to catch.

The blast went off with about three-quarters of a pound of powder in my hand, which consequently left me for dead in the bottom of the well, but shortly recovering and the neighbors assembling who hauled me up, and after getting bled and drinking a little spirits and water, felt tolerably well recovered, and in the course of eight days after, went to work; though feeling rather disagreeable, being both burnt and lame; however, I soon accomplished the well and for which I was well paid.

I then with some of my companions repaired to Wood's tavern, got groggy, after which was standing in the street, when a shop boy (Samuel Combs) threw a handful of lime mortar into my eyes, by which means notwithstanding every remedy connected with the assistance of doctors was made use of, I lost my right eye.

I applied to the boy's father for assistance, but never received any satisfaction. However, by the assistance of some worthy gentlemen in Lexington, viz. Messrs. James, William and Alexander Parker, John Bradford and William Leavy, there was a subscription raised for me, which assisted me much in my then distressed situation.

Mr. Castleman (tanner) of Woodford county, came to me, observing that his tanyard had gone dry, requesting me to go with him and procure him water. I accordingly went, but immediately on my arrival there was taken ill, owing to a cold I got, which struck into my eyes, but by the medical aid of Dr. Ridgely was soon relieved, and shortly after satisfied Mr. Castleman with water.

I then dug a well for Mr. Symmes near Woodford courthouse.

I fell in with a man of the name of Wright, with whom I agreed to dig wells in partnership. Going to Woodford courthouse we first commenced partnership in a drinking frolic, which continued until our money was all spent, and then observed by the landlord's looks that it was full time to decamp.

Fortunately a gentleman of the name of Sharp coming to the house, invited us home, where we were treated very politely.

Leaving there we started for Frankfort but my being taken with my old complaint (the bottle fever) occasioned my quartering under a tree. My comrade proceeded to the house of a Mr. Reeves, who kindly sent for me and had me conveyed to an outhouse prepared for my reception, where I got bled and continued for some days, being extremely well treated.

During my illness my comrade went on to Frankfort. For Frankfort I started likewise after recovering, but did not get beyond the crossroads before a Mr. Samuel made application requesting me to find water for him. Here proved a fine opportunity of proving the infallible doctrine of bletonism, there being at least 100 people present, a number of whom disbelieved the accuracy of said doctrine; but I soon opened their eyes to the truth of it, for laying off three different places which I marked, and being then carried into the house and there blindfolded, and then led out the same direction, I came within six inches of the above mentioned marks without the least variation, which correctness proved the infallibility of bletonism, and caused the astonished crowd to become proselyted to the doctrine.

I then proceeded to Frankfort, where I laid off a number of wells, and being called on by a Daniel Weisiger to judge a well he had on hand, which I did with my forket [forked] switch and condemned it, but on further examination found there was water to be got in his garden, and offered to dig him a well for $40, which he refused, though since acknowledged to me that he wished he had embraced my offer.

I then returned to Lexington. My fame as a well digger being established so thoroughly, that applications were coming to me every day from every part of the country, which encouraged me entering on a scene of intemperance, dissipation and extravagance, the consequence of which was going in debt in Lexington, particularly to Mr. Hugh MacIllvain, merchant in said town, to whom I owed $100.

It may perhaps be entertaining to the reader to know how I contracted part of this debt, which is as follows:

One court day in particular, getting a little as usual about half seas over, and dashing thro' and fro among the crowd, I happened to meet with an old woman and her daughter, informing them that I had been a widower nine years, and my attachment always being great for women, I promised them considerable presents provided the young one would grant me certain favors, to which she agreed.

I accordingly carried them to the store, where the young one first supplied herself with a handsome gownd pattern, and immediately slipped out the door; after which the old one received her fee, observing me talking to the storekeeper, she took the advantage and stepped out at the blind side of me, leaving me as usual in the lurch.

During the summer I made my home at a certain Mr. Kelley's, a brother well digger, convenient to whose house lived a young woman, to whom I got particularly attached. She being but indifferently clad, I supplied her with genteel apparel, and likewise paid a doctor for attending her during a severe fit of sickness, after recovering from which she married and left me as usual like the done-over tailor.

I was sent for by a Mr. Elisha Winter living on Tates creek, whom I assisted to dig a mill race, and for which I was well paid. After that, being sent for by a Mr. Anderson, who had a large cave on his land and was desirous of ascertaining whether or not there was water in it. I told him there was, but he wished to have it ascertained by someone going down.

A number being present, they all refused the disagreeable undertaking; however, for the honor of bletonism, I resolved on venturing down.

Immediately ropes and every necessary apparatus were prepared and then I made my gloomy exit; at the termination of my career I found what I was certain of before, a fine body of water, a bottle of which I brought up to satisfy the credulous expectants of my resurrection and doctrine—true I was much bruised in body and limbs, all of which I was willing to bear for the honor above mentioned.

I then commenced well digging for a certain Joel Hill, in part payment for which I agreed to take a wool hat, which I accordingly did, from a hatter, Mr. Hill sending his son with me when I got it.

But Mr. Hill neglecting to pay or rather would not pay for it, consequently it fell as usual upon Jonas.

I then started and came to a Mr. Redman's tavern, where I took a good jorum. I then proceeded on to Mr. Hubbard Taylor's, living in Clark county, for whom I dug a well and for which he honorably paid me.

At Strode's station[8] I met a soldier who was amongst those who took me prisoner, and whom I treated kindly, as he was in part the means of my continuing in a land of liberty.

Taking up goods in Cock and Lytle's store, to the amount of 18 pounds, I jogged on with them to Clark courthouse,[9] and there commenced a roaring frolic with a set of as jovial fellows as ever sat over a half pint of whiskey, amongst whom was a jolly Irishman, who cut as many didos as I could for the life of me; consequently he and I became the butts of the company, and at length began to wrestle, he being booted and spurred, and being likewise dexterous at the fun, had greatly the advantage of me, who had no shield against his steel but a thin pair of trousers and nothing to oppose his dexterity but strength.

However, by repeating our wrestling, I gained some knowledge of the art, and ultimately got the better of my old Hibernian, though not before I had my legs properly indented with the steel gaffs; the only recompence I could make for which was to lay him on his back in the fire to dry, as it were.

Here I exchanged all my goods for whiskey, then turned to jobbing about the town, and shewing Mr. Baker, the proprietor of the land, a number of places where water might be found. He kept me there a considerable time, endeavoring all in his power to acquire of me some knowledge of bletonism, after which he sent me off without either fee or reward.

I now started for Lexington, frolicking as usual, and took up goods in Thomas Hart's[10] store to the amount of four pounds eight shillings. I put up at Gabriel Poindexter's tavern, still continuing my intemperance until stopped in my career by a severe fit of sickness, in which I lay suspended between life and death for some considerable time, and were it not for the skill and kind attention of Dr. Ridgley, would never have recovered, it being full two months before I was capable of doing a stroke of work.

My first job after recovering was to wall a well for Mr. Wood, and by working for some time up to my middle in water, I unfortunately contracted a cold, which settled in my eyes, by which I became totally blind, but was restored to sight again by that humane and skillful physician, doctor Ridgley.

I now began to take a retrospect of my past life, considering maturely the sums of money and the precious time which I had misspent; therefore, resolving with the assistance of Divine Providence to amend my conduct, and be circumspect in my future deportment; as a prelude to which I commenced barkeeping for my landlord, Gabriel Poindexter, during the continuance of which no solicitations whatever could induce me to violate the bonds of sobriety.

In 1795 I commenced partnership in the stone quarrying business with a Mr. John Cock, and continued with him until the season for well digging came on, which was the means of my partly paying off my debts; for in this same John Cock I found a father, friend, and partner, a good citizen and an honest man.

After the conclusion of my partnership I commenced well digging and dug 19 that season, besides three more which I dug for captain John Fowler, quarried stone and walled them in.

In quarrying this stone I had the misfortune to be blown up again; for whilst I was ramming, the blast went off, blew the hammer out of one hand and the rammer out of the other to a considerable distance, however, I came off unhurt, a few scattering splinters excepted.

The winter coming on, I gave up well digging for the

season, and shortly after got acquainted with a young woman by the name of Susanna Bell (living in colonel Patterson's family) and to whom I was married by the Rev. Henry Toulmin.

The spring following, I purchased two lots of James Johnson, on one of which I built myself a new log house, into which I moved and in the course of the summer rented a quarry from John McConnel, and then carried on stone quarrying and lime burning very extensively.

I shortly thereafter engaged with captain Fowler to go to Bank lick to dig for salt water, under the superintendence of captain Alexander, and during my absence on the 11th day of October, had a son born, whom I called Henry Robert Shaw. I continued at the bank lick until driven away by a storm.

The year following, 1797, I engaged again with captain Fowler to go to the Bank lick and was to start on the first of August. I thought it best to move my family also, and accordingly sold my house and lot, and at an under price.

But when the time approached that we were to depart, captain Fowler, to my loss, was elected to congress, which entirely defeated my plan, which occasioned me being under the necessity of renting a house for myself and family.

I was at this time under the necessity of contracting an unavoidable debt, which was utterly out of my power to pay immediately. One of my creditors came to me and observed that a pretended friend of mine advised him to sue me.

This with some other crosses began to make me very uneasy, but my distresses reaching the ears of captain Fowler, he immediately came to town and desired me to bring him an account of the different debts which I owed; accordingly I did, and he became responsible for them all.

Here I cannot help digressing from the thread of my narrative to introduce an apostrophe of gratitude to that kind, that generous, and to me that incomparable friend; but panegyric must be thrown away on him; because his virtues as a man, as a citizen, and to sum up the whole, as an enlightened and disinterested patriot, are so universally known.

Colonel Patterson observing likewise the distressed situation of myself and family, humanely gave me a house to live in rent free, with as much fuel as I could consume, for which I shall ever retain a grateful sense.

On the 11th day of April, 1798, I had a daughter born to me, whom I called Nancy Robert Shaw. At the same time I entered into partnership with colonel Patterson, in the stone quarrying and lime burning business, and likewise leased two acres of land from him, for six years at 40 shillings per year.

On the 12th day of October, 1799, of glorious memory, I had a son born, whom I called John Robert Shaw, a chip of the old block; and with this pleasing intelligence, to you reader, I shall close this intteresting chapter.

Chapter 10

"I'll hoist away and make a smell—
And that's the way to dig a well."

I purchased a piece of land in Shelby county, in order to commence farming—accordingly built myself a house and moved there. I was led to believe that I should meet with good encouragement in my line of business in Shelby county, but I soon finished all that was to be done, and often wished myself back delving away in my old quarry again.

Getting tired, I sold my land and moved to near Shelbyville, on a farm belonging to colonel Lynch, who promised me continual employment, but in the course of seven weeks I finished all the work he had for me, and likewise all that was to be done in Shelbyville.

In 1801, on January 18th, I had a son born, whom I called William Robert Shaw; and in the fall following I returned to Lexington, with a firm determination never to move from it again.

I now rented a house of major Harrison, at 20 pounds per annum; and shortly after engaged with Messrs. Jordan, Wilkins & Co. to try for salt water in the Hanging Fork of Dick's river,[1] but without success.

I now considered that the rent I was paying was rather more than I could well afford in my present circumstances, I therefore provided myself with a house of lower rent; major Morrison demanding no more of me than was lawfully due for the time I continued in his house.

Shortly after, I went to dig a well eight miles from town, where I unfortunately was seized with the sciate, which continued on me ten months.

It was about this time that I leased a lot from Mr. Thomas Bodley[2] (the most fortunate day's work I ever did) upon conditions of making certain improvements, all of which I accomplished the first year.

Mr. Bodley likewise allowed me to open a quarry convenient to where I leased, paying six pence per perch for all the stone I quarried.

I now commenced stone quarrying without one shilling in my pocket, but the jade fortune who so often smiled as well as frowned on me, did not desert me in my present exigency; for three gentlemen, viz. Messrs. Archibald Logan, James Rose, and Christopher Smedley, stepped forward and rendered me every essential service which I stood in immediate need of—services which shall never be forgotten whilst John Robert Shaw continues to breathe the vital air.

I now drove on my business with encouragement and good success, my oldest son assisting me as much as his tender years would admit of, and by assiduity and industry was shortly able to hire as many hands as I wanted, and also to purchase a couple of pair of oxen, a cart and a wagon; and to crown all my good fortune, was blessed with another son, whom I called James Robert Shaw.

A contract being entered into between Messrs. Jordan, Wilkins & Co. with Messrs. Wilson, Ball & Co. for liberty to dig for salt water at a place known by the name of Knob Lick, for which purpose the gentlemen thought proper to employ me, where after working through different substances strongly impregnated with salt, I had the misfortune to be again blown up.

Mr. Young, superintender of the well, hearing the explosion from a neighboring house, immediately ran to the well and sent a man down to see what situation I was in. The man observing my brains running out cried out that it was not worth while taking me from where I was, as I was dead.

However, they soon hauled me up—had me conveyed to a cabin—sent to Danville with all possible speed for doctor McDowell,[3] who dressed my wounds.

I conceive it unnecessary enlarging any further on my deplorable situation: suffice it to say, that I lay 21 hours senseless, and in two days after was conveyed to Lexington. On my way through Danville I was treated with great humanity, which I shall never forget.

On the fourth day I arrived at my own house, and by the medical skill of doctor Fishback and the kind attention of my friends and neighbors, I continued mending until Christmas day, when I was setting with a few friends, and conversing on my happy deliverance, was instantly seized with a pain in my right eye, which occasioned me the most excruciating torment, connected with a very high fever, which induced doctor Fishback to bleed me sixteen times in ten hours.

In this distressed condition I remained for five days when my eye burst and immediately the pain left me.

This unhappy misfortune kept me from work for three months and five days, but during said time my kind and generous employers allowed me half pay, for which I hope the recompenser of all good will pay them in full.

As soon as I was able to do business my employers sent me to the well to superintend the business. But Mr. Young being there and ordering the boring in a manner which I told him would not do, and which after some perseverance he found it to be true.

Mr. Young is a very clever man, but knows nothing about well digging.

I left the Knob Lick again and came home to Lexington, where in order to attract public attention, I gave the following lines publicity:

I'll join unto the spade,
When on the rock the sledge is laid;
I'll hoist away and make a smell,
And that's the way to dig a well.

John R. Shaw, who now intends
To blow up rocks and dig in well,
Can water find by the new art;
So well the fresh, so well the salt.

Since conjurers became so wise,
In telling where salt water lies,
I hope I shall not be forsook,
I've try'd the art of Mr. Cook.

And to my friends I do declare,
A witch I never was before;
Before my master doth get rich,
Come unto me the art I'll teach.

No stipend of my friends I'll take,
I'll teach you all for friendship's sake;
And you that wish to dig salt wells,
May easily know that Shaw excels.

(Another)

In Lexington my friends may find
Me working at my trade;
In raising stone to suit your mind,
And digging with my spade.

All you that have my stone received,
And find them not to suit,
I'll haul the offals back again
And send a fresh recruit.

I can dig wells, you all well know
Good water I can find;
In spite of patent laws I'll shew,
For naught I will be kind.

Great contention long hath been,
Who can good water find;
But I'll insure, altho' unseen,
For all I am half blind.

Good lime I always have on hand,
Supplied you all can be
However great be your demand,
Come, friends, come unto me.

In all the branches of my trade
So punctual I will be,
It never shall by one be said,
John Shaw has cheated me.

As I am drawing towards the close of my narrative, I shall here insert the number of wells which I dug in the state of Kentucky, which must be a convincing proof to my fellow citizens that I have not been an idle performer on the grand theatre of life. The depth of said wells in feet, and the proprietors' names are likewise inserted as follows:

NAMES	FEET	NAMES	FEET
James Parker, Lexington	13	William Young	7
ditto ditto	11	Mr. Ferguson	13
John Bradford	9	Thomas Reed (Woodford)	9
Andrew Holmes	9	Philip Thurman, 2	15
William West	4	James Wallace (Fayette)	35

John R. Shaw 35
 ditto 17
George Adams 9
William Allen 8
John Boggs 13
Andrew Holmes 14
James Trotter 11
A public well 14
John McNair 5
Messrs. Morton & Beaty . . . 15

Messrs. Whitney & Mansill 14
John Postlethwait 18
 ditto 9
 ditto 29
A. MacIlvain 13
Mr. Parrish 13
Mr. McGowan 16
Mr. Coansi 11
Samuel R. Barr 12
George A. Weber 11
Robert Patterson 13
 ditto 17
John Ellison, 2 42
John Stillfield, 2 38
John McBain 29
John Smith 9
Edward West 15
Robert Campbell 25
Robert McCormick 24
Martin Hoagland 16
Nicholas Bright 20
Andrew Hare 20
John Fowler 15
 ditto 15
John Cock 9
Thomas Theoblad 12

Andrew McCalla 16
Ebenezer Platt 12
Michael Raber, 2 39
John Sprinkle 7
John Thompson 8
Mann Satterwhite, 2 54

John Kennedy 9
Hugh MacIlvain 10
Major Henry Scott 10
Robert Holmes (Lex.) 13
Major Henry Scott, 2 50
Mr. Long (Fayette) 15
Mr. McCann 26
John Dyer (Fayette) 10
John Jameson, 2 30
Lewis Castleman (Woodford)
. . . . 12
Josiah Mosley 3
John Sellars 3
Mr. Sims 3
Joseph McLain 3
Mr. Sims 19
Joel Hill (Madison) 19
 ditto 3
Hubbard Taylor (Clark) 20
George Taylor (Bason) 3
John Bucknor 3
John Gordon (Fayette) 9
John Fowler, 5 40
Jesse Guthrie (Lex.) 5
Mr. Young 7
State House (Frankfort) . . . 35
Major Love 57
Henry Ferguson 14
George Haytel (Lex.) 9
Nancarrow & Co. (Shelby) . 12
 ditto 18
Major Morrison & Co. 30
Widow Parker 22
Adam Keyser, 2 (Bason) . . . 17
David Stout 9
Mr. Morton 6
Gwinn R. Tompkins (Fayette)
. . . . 26
Col. Lynch, 2 (Shelby) 36
Adam Stout, 2 16
Mr. Shipman 3
A public well in Shelbyville 17
George Hansborough 14
Mr. Flournoy 6

Doctor Ridgley 29
Colonel Hart, 2 56
Peter January, sen. 31
For the seminary 17
Mr. Bosworth 26
Samuel Boyd (Fayette) 15
  ditto 30
John Higby 22
E. Hayden (Jessamine) 41
J. Wood 15
B. Roberts (Bason) 3
James Rose (Lex.) 10
Margaret Wood 23
Thomas Bodley 30
D. Payne (Fayette) 7
James Wilson (Lex.) 25
John Downing 7
Henry Clay 29
A. Logan 7
Mr. Morris, 2 (Jessamine) . . 11
David Stout (Lex.) 16
Buckner Thruston 29
Thomas Bodley 15
John Caldwell 31
John Jordan 25
William Huston 27
G. Keizer 13
William Leavy 14
Black Charless 2
Mr. Morton 12
John Campbell (Jessamine)   9
Benjamin Stout 14

Rice Smith 8
William Merriwether 16
John Reed (Shelby) 6
John Shipman 7
Dr. R. Henry (burnt house) 14
William Harris (Shelby) . . . 21
Mr. Smith (Bason) 3
Jesse Spears 3
Colonel Hart 36
C. Wilkins, 2 24
William Thompson 18
Liby & Co. 41
Anthony Blest 25
Andrew Price 12
Mr. Yeiser 13
Alexander Parker 9
Scott & Trotter 6
Trotter & Cross 13
Mr. Young 21
John Ficklin (Jessamine) . . . 22
S. G. Trotter (Lex.) 19
Ashton and Shread 22
Widow McNair 16
  ditto (Fayette) 10
John Brown (Lex.) 15
Mr. Thompson 16
Turner Morris (Jessamine) . 9
William Campbell (Bason) . 3
Mr. Crawford 12
Mason Lodge (Lex.) 23
Lewis Saunders 11

The whole amounting to 177 wells, and 2,608 feet, besides a number which I have dug within these four years, which I have kept no account of; also quarried 6,339 perch of stone and burnt 12,750 bushels of lime, and likewise dug and blew three mill seats and 150 rod of mill race.

The property which I have acquired by the aforesaid labor is five acres of land adjoining Lexington, on which is an excellent quarry, which with industry yields me annually a handsome profit.

On my lot I have made considerable improvements, such as a dwelling house, spring house, smoke house, wash house, a stable and wagon house, all of which I estimate at $2,000, and my lot and quarry at $2,000 more.

But in consequence of accumulating said property I have been equally if not more disabled in battling with the rocks than the gallant Nelson has been in battling against the enemies of his country,[4] as I have lost no less than one eye, four fingers, one thumb and seven toes.

But in taking a retrospect of my past life, it is a pleasing gratification to me that I have in many instances been useful to mankind in the line of my profession, and that I have through Providence been able to provide for my family with a handsome prospect of future support. These connected with the flattering hopes that I possess the goodwill of my fellow citizens, which I shall with assiduity endeavor to retain, are pleasing sources of consolation, which will eventually smoothe the rugged path of my peregrination through this life.

I shall now relate to my readers in the words of doctor Fishback, my then attending physician, as delivered by him to Mr. Bradford for publication, an account of my fourth and last time of having been blown up while digging a well for Mr. Lewis Saunders in Lexington:—

"Mr. Bradford,

"It may not be uninteresting to your readers, though distressing to humanity, to give publicity to one of the most dreadful misfortunes that perhaps has ever fallen to the lot of any individual—

"John R. Shaw, whose melancholy condition is the subject of this narrative, is a well digger and stone quarrier by trade, and is not less distinguished for his honesty, industry and usefulness, than for his accumulated evils (if such they may be called) which have pursued him for many years past.

"The 23rd of August I was called upon to visit him, being

informed that he had been blown up for the fourth time. On approaching his mangled body, it presented a spectacle unparalleled by anything which I have seen or known in the annals of men.

"The skull was fractured upon the frontal bone, a little to the right of the middle and just below the edge of the hair. In consequence of a very considerable depression, it became necessary to trepan the part by which a great number of small pieces of bone were taken out, and the depression entirely removed.

"The bone forming the wall of the external corner of the left eye was likewise broken, which was also removed. His right shin bone was very much shattered, the left arm was fractured in one place, with the loss of two fingers and the rest very much bruised; his right arm broken in two places, one just above the wrist and the other at the elbow, with a considerable injury to the hand; the skin upon the breast was very much bruised and cut, from which I inferred he was leaning nearly over the blast.

"His mouth, nose, skin and face, eyes and head were exceedingly wounded.

"Having several years before lost the use of his right eye, but little hopes now remained, should he recover, of his ever enjoying the advantage of sight again, as the surface of the remaining eyeball was considerably bruised and torn by a number of small pieces of stone.

"In addition to the above, his face was enormously swelled, and covered with blood, gunpowder and dirt, so that it was utterly impossible to recognize the lineaments of John Robert Shaw. The impression produced on my mind, from seeing his body lacerated in every part, is easier to be conceived than described. It may astonish the medical world to be informed that the use of the lancet was at no time necessary, nor was he at all delerious after recovering from the first shock.

"It may not be improper to observe that ultimately the wounds healed in the most friendly manner."

—*JAS. FISHBACK*

The deplorable situation of John R. Shaw, late
well-digger of Lexington, surrounded by his friends and
distressed family—23d August, 1806.

Here, reader, picture to yourself my pitiable situation; a
wife with a numerous progeny bemoaning my sad condition,
whose cries and situation occasioned more anguish to my heart
than my excruciating torture did that of pain to my feeling.

But I cannot in justice refrain my pen from observing that
the unremitting, skillful and assidious attention of my sur-
geons, doctors Fishback, Dudley and Warfield, connected with
the generous contributions of my neighbors were an innate
source of satisfaction to me, and a great means of alleviating
those acute sensations which I then laboured under and which
at this side of eternity shall never be erased from my grateful
bosom.

I will now take leave of my candid reader, if any reader
should have patience to accompany me so far, by endeavoring to
warn those who are entering into life against those follies and

vicious vices, which are laid down in the preceding pages, and which the author was led into, from the strong propensity of his nature, to that depravity which is always indiginous to us frail mortals.

Through all the career of my folly, vice and intemperance, I made it a point never to lose sight of industry; from which source I now derive my present advantages in pecuniary concerns; with the pleasing prospect of an ample support for myself and family during my declining years.

Therefore, I recommend industry to my youthful readers, which is the law of our being; it is the demand of nature . . .

And now I wish to observe that in whatever I have said in the style of direction and advice, I meant only to offer, not to obtrude; to submit, not to dictate.

John R. Shaw

THE END

Appendix

Subscribers' Names, 1807

Lexington

William Dunlap
David Williamson
Ely Rosell
Bledsoe Wright
Thomas C. Thompson
Thomas Boaze
Samuel Price
Samuel Downing
John Fisher
Phil. Thomas
Wm. Smith
Thomas Sthreshly
D. McNair
John W. Honey
Thomas Chamberlain
Ebenezer Farrow
Patterson Bain
John Brand
Francis McMordie
Thomas Stevenson

Joseph H. Hervey
Edward Howe
Nathaniel Morrison
Thomas Hatton
John Cock
D. Dodge
John Whaley
William Huston
John Lieby
Thomas M. Prentiss
C. Coyle
Will. Morton
John Frazer
John Johnston
John F. Bell
Alexander Frazer
J. Hart
Wm. Sthreshly
S. William Megowan
J. Boyd

Luke Usher
Benjamin Grimes
William Todd
John Ogilby
James Condon
John Kieser
Matthew Kennedy
Allen Davis
Isaac Reid
Samuel D. Stout
Francis Lockett
Jabez Vigus
James John
Alexander Parker
Thomas Beettor
Thomas Blythe
Thomas Q. Roberts
H. Taylor, Jr.
Cary Nichols
John Rigglesworth

Thomas Railey, Jr.
Anthony B. Shelby
Thomas Irwin
William Todd
E. Warfield
William Allen
Alexander Patrick
Robert Bradley
J. P. Wagnon
Charles Wickliffe
William West
John Downing
Gabriel Lewis
John Postlethwaite
Nat. G. S. Hart
John L. Martin
Joshua Wilson
George Russell
Ab. S. Barton
Robert R. Hall
David Todd
Lloyd Posey
A. LeGrand
C. Kieser
George M. Bibb
David M. Sharbe
C. Govett
L. Castleman, Jr.
J. Starkey
David Maccoun
William T. Barry
Thomas M. Gist
John M. Morton
Matthew J. Jouett
William T. Blanton
James Hickman
Solomon Slaback
C. Wilson
James Bliss
John Steele
John D. Young
S. K. Blythe
Henry Terrass
Robert McCormick

John Jordan, Jr.
James Coleman
Peter I. Robert
Isaac Yarnell & Co.
Richard Monks
Curtis Field
Andrew Armstrong
W. Warfield
Jacob Claar
H. MacIlvain
John J. Crittenden
Joseph Day
Robert Campbell
B. F. Gore
Robert Bywaters
John Fleming
John H. Hesler
William Tyree
John F. Carter
William Bobb
T. Dunn
John Arthur
John Springle
John Bobb
Henry Ball
N. Prentiss
James Cownover
W. M. Nash
Robert Grinstead
Hiram Shaw
James Montgomery
Joriah Brady
Samuel Biles
Richard Willis
Craven Peyton
Jonathan Smith
David Blackwell
Charles Humphreys
Elijah Oliver
Samuel E. Watson
John M. Young
Matthew Woods
James Richardson
Jefferson Boggs

Thomas Royle
Thomas T. Barr
Daniel Bradford
N. S. Prentiss
Edward Prentiss
Peter Paul, Jr.
Wm. W. Worsley
Wm. Stewart
William Thompson
William Holmes
Samuel McChesney
Richard Barry
David Woodruff
Henry Shindelbower
David Irwin
Benjamin McDaniel
J. McDaniel
John Knox
Dudley Gatewood
David Stout
N. Burrowes
Alexander M. Edmiston
William Scott
Samuel Ayres
David Sutton
Richard Holding
Matthew Elder
Elijah Noble
B. Bosworth
Eng. Yeiser
Samuel T. Davenport
E. Sharp
Craven T. Peyton
Benj. Davis
John L. McCullough
J. G. Trotter
Robert Campbell, Jr.
Robert A. Sturgus
Matthew Shryock
John Wrigglesworth
John Harris
James Rose
Isaac Holmes
Isaac Reid

Lilburn Boggs
John Carty
James Robert
John Frazer
Samuel Smeadley
Barry & Garrett
John Todd, Jr.
Maddox Fisher
Lewis Saunders
Caleb B. Wallace
John H. Lonckart
William Long
William Pritchartt
A. Montgomery, Jr.
Thomas Bodley
F. Bradford, Jr.
George Mansell
Mr. Blanchard
John F. Wagnon, Jr.
Warner Hawkins
William Cavin
Jo. Oliver
James Morrison
Richard Blanton
Richard Stephens
Robert Macnitt
Andrew McCalla

Reuben Cluff
L. Young
James Reed
Henry Clay
Jeremiah Douglass
Robert Stout
Thomas J. Dickinson
Samuel VanPelt
James Fishback
John May
William Gray
George Norton
Robert Dudley
A. W. Rollins
Andrew F. Price
Charles Wilkins
Thomas McBarney
L. B. Hawkins
John Whitney
Norban B. Cooke
John W. Ryan
Lyndon Comstock
James B. January
Henri I. I. Robert
Wm. Hart
Henry K. Lewis
Lexington Library

John M. Boggs
E. Palmer
Lindsay Blanton
Archibald Campbell
Thomas C. Graves
Gabriel Tandy
New. Crockett
Benj. W. Dudley
Joseph Hawkins
William Hanson
David F. Todd
Daniel B. Price
Trotter & Tilford
Moses Cox, Jr.
Joseph Hudson
John Wyatt
William Henry
Martin Hawkins
Benjamin Temple
Joseph Wier
H. Johnson, US army
Miss New
Miss Parker
Miss Bradford
Miss Warfield
Miss Blair
Miss Austin
Miss Hughes

Fayette County, Kentucky

Alexander Willis
Jacob McConathy
David Worley
Thomas Hill
Fielding Smithey
William Gist
Edward Payne
William Steel
G. R. Tompkins
John McDowell
Matthew Flournoy
Chas. Patrick
Absalom Bainbridge

Daniel Bryan
James Wood
William Rowan
William L. Meredith
Reuben Hudson
James Curd
William Vaughan
John Smith
John Nolen
Jonathan Jewel
Wm. Roffe
James True, Jr.
Ludwell Carey

William Meredith
Jesse Calvert
John Bostick
James Hamilton
Benjamin Moore
John Murphy
Jammey Payne
Adam Winn
John Bryant
Moses S. Hall
James Casterphen
Elijah Foley
Moses Moore

Edmund Cullin
Jacob Laudeman
John Dudley
Thomas MacIlroy
Stark Gilliam
John Haggerty
Newbolt Crockett
Wm. McConnell
Clement Ferguson
Larkin Price
U. J. Devore
Wm. Kenny
John Dillard
Wm. Stone
James Caruthers
Charles Tair
Josiah Guess
Stark Johnson
Thomas Gutar
Benjamin Laughlin
B. Gaves

Simon Laughlin
Anderson Miller
Robert McNair
John Irwin
James McConnell
Benjamin Johnson
Robert Kay
Robert Simpson
John Gardner
Harbin Moore
James R. Cooley
Andrew Armstrong
James McDowell
David Steel
John VanPelt
E. Tudor
John G. Boyer
Thomas Nicholds
James Lawrence
Whitehead Leonard
Elijah Grimes

John Murphy
Benjamin Smith
Henry Payne
James Davis
Nathan Payne
John Bostick
John Watts
Benjamin Moore
Eliza Blair
William W. Sutton
Wm. Higgins
James Lindsay
Josiah Lee
James Tracy
George Armstrong
J. Spangler
John Nichols
Matthew Rule
George Rogers
John Boyd
Richard Higgins

Frankfort

Edmund Hardman
Thomas V. Loofberry
B. Hickman
Elisha Herndon
B. G. Farrar
Ambrose Jeffries
John M. Scott
Robert Brenham
Thomas S. Windgate
John Glover
Thomas Tunstall
George G. Davis
Spils be Daniel
Oliver Brown
Thomas Hickman
Philip Bush
John Eidson
Thornton A. Posey
Francis Ratliff
Isham Talbot

John G. Meaux
Ezra Richmond
John Yeatman
Wm. Samuel
W. S. Waller
Stephen Young
Owen Reiley
Paschal Hickman
Joseph M. Street
George Greer
Achilles Sneed
Walker During
John McKinley
John Cunningham
Eliz. L. James
Mathew Clarke
John D. Richardson
Daniel Winter
Edmund Bacon
William Taylor

J. A. Mitchell
Isaac Scoffield
James Johnson
Wm. Bryan
Langston Bacon
Wm. White
Reuben Runyan
Samuel Throckmorton
Charles Sprowl
Adam Caldwell
Thomas Hughes
Daniel Weisiger
Thomas Long
Simon Kenton
John Logan
Mark Hardin
John Younger
T. Y. Bryant
Christopher Greenup
Charles Springer

R. C. Anderson, Jr.
Samuel H. T. Young
Samuel Allison
John Campbell

Wm. Medcalf
Mathew Talbot
William Berry
Jephthah Dudley

Robinson Graham
Jas. S. H. Roberts
Th. Carneal
Edmund Hardman

Franklin County, Kentucky

Wm. Fenwick
James Gale
Presley Oliver
Thos. P. Major
Rev. Samuel Shannon
Hugh Innes
Isaac Keller
Reuben Samuel
Seneca McCrackin
Alexander Macy
Charles L. Nall
John Castleman
John Price
Reuben Samuel
Philip Taylor
Wm. Bourne
Edmund Vaughan
Edmund Ware
Thomas Carneal
Edmund Waller
John Crutchfield

James Davis
Wm. Trigg
Francis Graham, Jr.
Wm. G. Brown
John Bacon
Thomas Bryan
Samuel Ware
George Jordan
Paul Faut
Cornelius Fenwick
Thomas Blanton
Wm. L. Cox
Wm. Owen
Philemon Rowzer
Geo. Smith
Wm. Samuel
Daniel James
Thomas Major
Hugh McCreary
Isaac E. Gano
Robert Russell

Archibald Hamilton
Lyddell Bacon
Richard McGraw
John Rennick
Lewis J. Major
John Edwards
Larkin Gatewood
James Blair
Wm. Hubbell
John Jackson
John Madison
John J. Felix
George Madison
Wm. Ware
Wm. Smithe
Webb Haydon
Ambrose White
Hugh Alexander
John Lightfoot
John Sebree
Wm. Marshall

Versailles, Kentucky

C. C. Conway
Richard Dictum
Joseph Davidson
John Francisco
Benj. Clarke
Daniel Spangler

Jesse Tannehill
Simon Smith
William George
Geo. W. McClary
Isaac Woodbridge
Henry Stone

Andrew Ross
Joseph Dictum
Wm. Gatewood
Joseph George
Robert Clarke
John McKinney

Woodford County, Kentucky

Lewis Marshall
John Guthrie
James Bell
John Blanton

Wm. Woods
John L. Head
Richard Fox
Thos. Bell

Mathew Gale
Moses Hawkins
Keene O'Hara
—Blanton

Wm. Dailey   James Guthrie   Wm. Steele
Wm. Herndon   John O'Bannon   David Castleman
George Yellott   John Ramsey   Francis Allen
Wm. Rice   Samuel Berry

Richmond, Kentucky

Thomas C. Howard   James Talbott   David C. Irvine
H. D. Cock   Benj. Milner   John Burnam
Geo. Shackleford   Wm. Conden   Michael Wallace
John Chapman   Ezekiel H. Field   Samuel McMahan
Thomas I. Stewman   John Grugate   Richard P. Hose
David King   Andrew Haynes   Adam Noble
George Morris   Joseph Morris   Samuel Logan

Shelby County, Kentucky

William W. Cooke   Jacob Castleman   Giles Smith
Thomas Ellis   Noble Nash   Stephen Ellis
Robert Miller   Wm. Tool   John Goe
Jesse Lewis   Wm. Adams   James H. Ficklin

Madison County, Kentucky

Abraham Hammond   Edward Durbin   William Williams
Joseph Hyatte   Daniel Green   Merel Emery
McNemar Adams   Baxter Cooper   Hugh Brown
Higgason Grubbs   Samuel Kelly   James Barnett
Archibald Curle   Alexander Garten   Jacob Patton
Ben Scribner   Saschel Cooper   Samuel Turner
John Stevenson   John Boggs   Richard Ransome
Charles Cothern   Robinson Jameson   Will. Hervey
Thomas Crews   Elijah Morin   Wallis Estill, Jr.
J. W. Walker   Robert Rhodes   John Reid, Jr.
William Chenault (sen.)   Lewis Gillespie   Abner Kelly
James Hockerday   Ephraim Wayne   Joshua Quinn
Ebenezer Dickey   G. H. Bullard   John Bennett
Jacob Seburn   Schuyler Burnett   William Woods
Samuel Fox (sen.)   James Hatter   George Humes
William Beele   John White B. H.   Samuel Taylor
John Kelly   Nicholas Hawkins   James Stone
Reuben Hatton   Henry White   Thomas White
Elias Simmons   Patrick Woods   Joseph Durbin

James Hendricks
Josias Phelps
Wm. Clarke
Joseph Lynes
Peter Woods
Elijah Smallwood

Samuel Campbell
Thomas Cox
Joseph Delany
Robert Miller
Henry Brooks
John Durbin

Wm. Barnett
Jesse Jones
Joseph Patrick
John Wagle
Thomas Dozer

Jessamine County, Kentucky

John Wallace
Shadrach Moore
John Thomas
Andrew Saygar
John Kirley

Joseph Crockett
James Lockett
Jacob Keller
Nicholas Lewis
Thomas Reynolds

Joseph Roberts
Wm. Hornbuckle
J. Marrs
Jacob Smith

Scott County, Kentucky

Thomas Bond
James Gough
Samuel Emison
James Temblin
Thomas W. Hawkins
James Johnson

A. Mitchell
Wm. Henry
John Sterrett
James Barnes
Jas. Wood Hawkins

Humphrey Sparks
Josiah Pitts
Dempsey Carnel
William Massie
Strother Jones Hawkins

Bairdstown (Bardstown), Kentucky

John Rowan
P. Quinton
James Coleman
Peter W. Grayson
Benj. Chapeys
Thomas Roberts
Nathaniel Wickliffe
Andrew Aynes
Thomas Crutcher
Charles Morehead
J. B. Strother

John Speed
Robert C. Hall
Thomas W. Hynes
L. Yeiser
Wm. Watkins
Andrew Buchanan
E. S. Thomas
John Webb
Lewis Quigley
Thomas Headon

Levi Brashear
John McMacklin
Abner Hynes
Jacob Tabler
T. C. Brashear
Robert Nickeson
T. B. Reed
Samuel Carpenter
Wm. Crutcher
T. C. Slaughter

Danville, Kentucky

John Cochran
Frederick Yeiser
John Warren

Thomas Hiter
Richard Davenport
Benj. Smith

Robert Culton
Thomas Moseby
John Y. Hiter

Isaac Alspaugh   John F. Rasor   James Harlan
Wm. Owens   James Clemens, Jr.   Michael Hope
William Green   Joseph Brewer   Wm. Cruthfield

Harrodsburg, Kentucky

Horace Smith   George Thompson   Wm. Phenego
Harrison Munday   William Hord   Isaac Sutton
George Smith   G. Thompson

Jefferson County, Kentucky

Richard P. Banks   Anthony Miller   John T. Gray
John C. Beeler   David L. Ward   Richard Taylor, Jr.

Mt. Sterling, Kentucky

Wm. Chiles   N. Hodge   John Mason, Jr.
William Reid   Henry Coffer   Asa K. Lewis
George Howard   Micajah Harrison   John Young
John Peebels   Wm. Calk, Jr.   John Smith
James Crawford   Jeremiah Davis   David Trimble
James S. Magowan   John Mills   Archibald MacIlvain
Joseph Simpson

Fleming County, Kentucky

William Hodge   Thos. Dougherty   Wm. Godard
A. C. Ballard   Robt. Turner   Jas. Dunlap
Gabriel Evans   Henry Bruce   Sam Kirkpatrick
James McKensie   John Lyans   Thomas Scott
David Blue

Clark County, Kentucky

Sam M. Taylor   Richard Graham   N. S. Dallam
Jas. Spilman   Geo. Webb   J. Rawlings
Arch. Bristow   Valentine Crawford   Benj. Mallory
H. Taylor   Wm. N. Lane   Geo. Stevenson
James Boyle   John Thompson   Mathew Thompson
Henry Daniel   Jno. Bailelle   Mordecai Gist
Richard Stevens   Jno. Sudduth   Jno. W. Hinde
John Pearson   Isaac L. Baker   Branch Tanner
Jas. Ritchie   W. R. Brasfield   Philip Richardson

Washington County, Kentucky

Wm. Murphy	John M. Lee	Henry Kenyon
George Morton	Francis Taylor	Charles Ward
John Johnston	Thomas Forman	B. B. Stith
Sam. Baldwin	Jas. Dimmett	Wm. B. Lurtey
John Wilson	David Evans	Marshall Key
James W. Coburn	Walker Reid	Edward Settle
John Howison	Charles Reiley	John Keets
William Parker	Wm. Worthington	Eli Harris
A. K. Marshall	Wm. Branurgh	John Chambers
Henry Lee	D. Vertner	B. Bayles
Ezekiel Forman	Wm. H. B. Philips	George Corwine
Isaac Beckley	Samuel Smith	Lawson Dobyns
Thomas Sloo		

Paris, Kentucky

William Ford	Wm. Paton	Mathew Duncan
David Holt	Oba S. Timberlake	David Hanway
John Carnagy	Michael Litton	James Humphrey
Demovelt Talbott	Roger Williams	Josiah Culp
Caleb E. Irvin	Geo. Hopkins	John Vaile
Jacob A. Lane	James Tillet	Wm. Rogers
Jacob Coyle	Samuel Love	Henry P. Brown
David Clarkson	Josiah Ashurst	Tunstall Cox
Henry Betterton	Archibald Beall	Wm. Scott
Wm. Garrard	Joseph Smith	

Millersburg, Kentucky

George Selden	Sam G. Mitchell	Philip B. Smoot
Thomas Baker	Hugh Duffin	Wm. Mitchell
Isaac Hall	William Holladay	

Bourbon County, Kentucky

John Porter	John Steele	Robert Hand
Abraham Jones	Robert Scrogin	Jones & Cummings

Harrison County, Kentucky

John Kelso	Benson Fixworthy	Ge. Kirkpatrick
W. Moore	Milton Forsythe	Jacob Powers

Charles Hutchinson	Jacob Kookendorfer	Robert Ellison
Thomas Martin	George Smiser	John Wallace
Hugh Newell	Charles Kelso	Robert Houston
Wm. Kasey	J. Coleman	David Humphreys
Wm. Coleman	Perry Crosthwait	Joel Fraizer
Jarret Wall	Allen Woods	Thomas Holt
Anthony Thomas	Joseph Walker	Isaac Ruddell

Greenup County, Kentucky

Charles N. Lewis	George Knox	Jacob Neal
Wm. Morrison	Terrance McGrath	Edmund Carey
Reuben Fitzgerald	Abraham Goble	Jacob M. Ham
John Young	Richard Hailey	Thomas Chaire
Benj. S. Miller	Nimrod Canterbury	Geo. Smith, Jr.

Russellville, Kentucky

John Todd	Joseph Ficklin	Joseph Ficklin
Willis Morgan	Armistead Morehead	Urbin Wing
Mathew Lodge	Andrew Caldwell	Wm. W. Thompson
Frederick Wadsworth	John Sharp	Wm. Carson
Robert A. McCabe	Spence Curd	Leonard White
Geo. W. Whitaker	Samuel H. Curd	John B. Truitt
John P. Oldham	Richard Curd	Joseph Hamilton
Wiley I. Barner	Smith Dallam	John Adams
Wm. W. Whitaker	Thos. G. Granfield	Reuben Ewing
Thomas Rigg	John Howell	John Reed
Samuel Wilson		

Christian County, Kentucky

| Jas. H. McLaughlin | John Campbell | Robert Coleman |
| Benj. P. Campbell | Wm. Ford | |

Lincoln County, Ky.—Langstick McVey and John Gibson
Campbell County, Ky.—Enos Rust and Josiah Brady
Pendleton County, Ky.—Francis Flournoy and Francis W. Sterne
Henry County, Ky.—James Bartlett, Peter Banta, Samuel Nelson, and Oliver Hughes
Henderson County, Ky.—Samuel G. Hopkins and Nathan Anderson
Gallatin County, Ky.—James C. Sneed, George Craig, and Wm. Stafford
Clay County, Ky.—Hugh White and James Kincaid
Adair County, Ky.—George Worley and James Tilford

Knox County, Ky.—Benjamin Chestnut
Garrard County, Ky.—J. M. McQuie
Green County, Ky.—Jas. Galloway
Shepherdsville, Ky.—Wm. Pope
Hartford, Ky.—Joseph Dunlap
Barren County, Ky.—Alexander Adair

Lancaster, Pa.

A. Bausman	Frederick Baker	Jacob Kirk
Benjamin Grimler	Anthony Albright	Owen Bruner, Jr.
Jacob Sharer	Geo. Hoffman	Michael Berger
Mathew Davis	Jacob Duchman	Wm. B. Ross, Esq.
John Rohrer, Jun.	Samuel Light	John Buckwalter
John Graul	John Mayler, Jun.	Reuben Sneather
Henry Buckwalter	George Withers	Frederick Grout
Wm. Barnett, Esq.	Wm. Feree	Joel Lightner
Wm. Henderson	John Riddle	John Eichelholtz
Martin Miller	Matthew Irwin	John Jordan
John Bausman	Wm. Bausman, Esq.	Benj. Shuler
Jacob Pickel	Samuel Garber	John Hamilton
John Sleter	Samuel Diller	Henry Carpenter
Christian Herr	Jacob Pennock	Geo. Bressler
Thomas Wallace	James Paight	Philip Ferris
J. Andrew Shulze	Evan Green	Henry Saiger
David Barnum	John Mathiot	John Bachman

Philadelphia, Pa.—M. Cake, No. 106 N. Front St.; John Berryhill and Wm.
     Wiltberger
Charleston, Va. (W. Va.)—John Humphreys
Washington City (Washington, D.C.)—R. Elliott
Baltimore, Md.—Jacob Boyer and Richard Ridgely
Blount County, Tenn.—John Lyle, M.D.
St. Genevieve (Up. Lou.) (Louisville)—Andrew Miller
Lebanon, Ohio—John McLean
Boston, Mass.—A. F. Giraud, French consul, and H. Newman, Jr.

Chillicothe, Ohio

Thomas Scott	Thomas S. Hinde	Isaac Evans
James McDougal	Jacob Thompson	N. Willis
John Edmiston	Oliver Simpson	John McDougal
Peter Parcels	Geo. H. Smith	A. Stephenson
Wm. Long	Catherine Wood	Nancy D. Tiffin
Nathaniel Massie	Samuel James	

Cincinnati, Ohio

Samuel J. Brown	Andrew Dunseth	Henry Looker
James H. Looker	Jacob Broadwell	Stephen Gano
Wm. McFarland	John Nimmo	James Conner

(signed) D. Bradford, printer, Lex., Ky.

Notes

Introduction

1. Other public notices concerning Shaw: The Lexington city fathers announced in the *Gazette* that Shaw had furnished stone for the city's new market house. Shaw's name and his occupations as well digger and stone cutter also appeared in two versions of the city directory in 1806.

2. Daniel Bradford was a printer and publisher of the *Kentucky Gazette* from 1802 to 1809. His father, John Bradford, founded the newspaper in August, 1787.

3. The only complete copy of Shaw's edition [at this writing in 1970] is in the University of Kentucky Libraries' Special Collection. It had belonged to Judge Samuel J. Wilson of Lexington, and upon his death it went to the university. The Filson Club of Louisville has an incomplete copy.

4. See *Statutes at Large of Pennsylvania*, vol. 14, p. 478.

Chapter 1

1. It was not possible to document Shaw's birth in England.

2. If the time elements are correct between Shaw's enlistment and arrival in America, he must have enlisted at the very beginning of 1777,

or even late 1776. His age at enlistment was probably under fifteen and a half.

3. This is a ribbon, used especially as a decoration.

4. This was an instrument of punishment better known as cat o'nine tails.

5. This was off Gravesend Bay in Brooklyn, New York.

6. This is now Elizabeth, New Jersey.

Chapter 2

1. The Tappan Massacre is well documented in the history of the American Revolution.

2. This was the Hudson River.

3. This is a reference to General "Mad Anthony" Wayne's victory at Stony Point on July 16, 1779.

4. This is a reference to Wayne's defeat at Paoli, Pennsylvania, in September 1777.

5. This was Lieutenant Colonel Banastre Tarleton.

6. This is now Moncks Corner, South Carolina.

7. This is a reference to General Benjamin Lincoln, who surrendered on May 12, 1780.

8. The Ninety Six referred to here is 2½ miles from the present Ninety Six, South Carolina.

9. This surprise attack is usually referred to in history books as the Battle of Fishing Creek, which took place about 38 miles from Camden on the Wateree or Catawba rivers.

10. This was Brigadier General Daniel Morgan.

11. The battle at Cowpens was on January 17, 1781.

Chapter 3

1. This was General Henry "Lighthorse Harry" Lee.

2. General Nathaniel Greene replaced General Gates in command.

3. Shaw's total service under Webster appears to have begun about January 1777, and concluded with a year as a prisoner of war. His service to the Crown ended in March 1782.

4. A Portuguese coin, the johannes, was worth a little more than $8. The coins were used in the colonies and were called "joes."

5. This is now Lititz, Pennsylvania.

6. The ruins of Coleman's furnace, built in 1781, are at Colebrook, Pennsylvania. Here were made the tin-plate stoves once used widely in farm homes.

7. This crossroads was in the vicinity of the present village of Sporting Hill, Pennsylvania.

8. This is Little Chickies Creek. It empties into Chickies Creek between West Hampfield and Mount Joy, Pennsylvania. The name was taken from the first half of the Indian word *chickiswalunga*, "place of the crayfish."

9. Carlisle Barracks is the oldest activated military installation in the United States. It was opened in 1757. In 1990, the Army War College is still in operation there. What was formerly the Dunham Army Hospital is now the Dunham U.S. Army Health Clinic.

10. This is a reference to General Arthur St. Clair's defeat on November 3, 1791. Butler was killed at Miami, Ohio, November 4, 1791. See chapter 4, note 3.

Chapter 4

1. There were two places in Pennsylvania called Standing Stone. Standing Stone Township near Towanda was named for a landmark. The other was an Indian village named for an upright stone column the Indians regarded with superstitious veneration. The Indians left the village in 1754, taking the stone with them. Huntingdon was laid out on the site, but settlers persisted in calling it Standing Stone. Shaw was referring to the Huntingdon site.

2. This celebration in 1782 was not necessarily on July 4. Among previous Independence Day celebrations, Carlisle Barracks observed one as late as October 29.

3. Richard Butler, called by erroneous titles (even by General Washington), was stationed at Carlisle Barracks from 1776 to 1783. Although at times he commanded in the field, he served also as president of a general court-martial that sat continuously at Carlisle Barracks from 1779 to 1783. The post was deactivated in 1784, but in May 1791, Butler was again there to reactivate it. At all times while there he appeared on the officer roster as a brigadier general, and was promoted to major general in late summer when he reached Ohio and became second in command to General Arthur St. Clair.

4. This was McAllister's town, near the southern border of central Pennsylvania. It was a haven for deserters and criminals.

5. Conewago was west of Lancaster, Pennsylvania, in the Conewago Valley.

6. Carlisle was laid out in 1751. Iron furnaces and limestone quarrying were important in early days. It began with five dwellings and a small fort.

7. This is Dickinson College, founded in 1783.

8. This is LeTort Spring.

9. This is Conodoguinet Creek. References in 1731 called it "Conegogwainet." The Oneida Indians called it "Conogoginet."

10. Conestoga, once an Indian village where in 1763 a number of friendly Indians were murdered by the "Paxton gang," was southwest of Lancaster.

11. Pequea, a village in Lancaster County, was frequently referred to by Shaw as "Pickway."

Chapter 5

1. Because of financial difficulties Congress was unable to pay the troops, and Pennsylvania soldiers marched on Philadelphia in 1783 "to obtain prompt settlement of their accounts."

2. This is Chambersburg.

3. Concerning Peddlehouzer, Jeanne H. Mahler of the Public Documents Department of the Free Library of Philadelphia, said, "We have been unable to find the location of this town. A call to the Historical Society of Pennsylvania also yielded no results."

4. This route was from Gap, Pennsylvania to Newport, Delaware.

5. Christiana bridge (spelled both "Christian" and "Christein" by Shaw) was at Christiana, Delaware. It was built in 1686. The town once was a shipping point between Delaware and Philadelphia. The bridge, often referred to by travelers as "Christeen bridge," also was a starting point for a semi-weekly packet service to Philadelphia. By 1787 the bridge was taken out of service.

6. This was one of the Pennamite-Yankee wars between Pennsylvania and Connecticut over disputed lands in the Wyoming Valley. Although by the Decree of Trenton in 1782 Congress decided in favor of Pennsylvania, skirmishes continued until Connecticut formally relinquished its claim in 1800.

7. The companies, already in Philadelphia and east of the Schuylkill River, did not cross that river en route to the town of Wyoming. The river's source is in Schuylkill County, a considerable distance west-

southwest of Easton. Shaw, therefore, must have believed the Lehigh River was the Schuylkill, since the former would have to be crossed to get to Wyoming.

8. There are two such places in Pennsylvania. One is the dense hemlock forests that surround the village of Shade Gap, north of McConnelsburg. The other is a large, marshy plateau with a dense expanse of pines and undergrowth at Belle Meadow (no post office) about fourteen miles south of Scranton. The latter was the "Shades of Death" that Shaw knew.

Chapter 6

1. Although no weather records are available for 1784, the president of the Wyoming Historical Society said he believes this incident could have occurred. R.E. Simmermacher, meteorologist at the Wilkes-Barre Scranton Airport Weather Bureau, Avoca, Pennsylvania, commented, "The winters were generally hard and long and sometimes the area had a late spring. These people could have been found in a frozen condition in May. The cabin was probably deep in the woods where spring sunshine would not reach. Approximately 80 years ago, a lumberman was found late in the spring frozen to death in our area." Recorded low temperatures for May in northeastern Pennsylvania include 18 degrees at Muncy Valley and 19 degrees at Mount Pocono. R.W. Schloemer, deputy director of climatology for the Environmental Science Services Administration, Silver Spring, Maryland, said that "according to historical accounts the winter of 1783–84 was unusually cold and one of the longest ever" and "that the weather could have caused the tragedy seems entirely possible."

2. Most of the taverns mentioned in the Philadelphia area are documented in the Free Library of Philadelphia.

3. One version of this battle is that in January 1778, a flotilla of kegs filled with gunpowder was floated down the Delaware River from Bordentown, New Jersey, with a view of their reaching the British fleet, which the patriots thought was anchored in an exposed position at Philadelphia. Francis Hopkinson, Philadelphia poet and jurist, further annoyed the British with a satirical ballad called "The Battle of the Kegs." The last of the twenty-two stanzas went thus:

> The cannons roar from shore to shore;
> The small arms loud did rattle.
> Since wars began, I'm sure no man
> E'er saw so strange a battle.

4. Fort McIntosh was in Beaver County, Pennsylvania. It was built on

the site of the present town of Beaver on the Beaver River, a northern tributary of the Ohio.

5. This was the Conestoga Creek.

Chapter 7

1. Hannahstown once was the "capital of western Pennsylvania," to which the men traveled long distances to vote. Hostile Indians and Tories destroyed it in 1782. The later Hannahstown was about a mile north of the old one and four miles north of Greensburg. Shaw must have traveled through the first Hannahstown site since it was on the old Forbes Road to Pittsburgh.

2. General James O'Hara, an army contractor and industrial promoter, is said to be Pittsburgh's first industrialist. There, in 1797, with two partners, he opened a glass manufacturing plant that was the first to use coal in the process.

3. Shaw may have been only indicating a direction. Or, he might have believed that the west bank of the Ohio River at that point was in Virginia. Both Virginia and Pennsylvania claimed the land there until 1779. A permanent boundary was agreed on in 1782. In 1784–85 the Mason-Dixon line was extended westward from Maryland to its present terminus and in the following year the western boundary was drawn due north to Lake Erie.

4. "Shirtee" was and is Chartiers Creek, which empties into the Ohio opposite Brunot Island on the way down to McKees Rocks from Pittsburgh.

5. McKees Rocks is a rocky ledge along the river opposite the town of McKees Rocks.

6. Bryan Station, northeast of Lexington, Kentucky, was defended against a Canadian and Indian attack in August 1782, in which the women at the station are said to have played an important role.

7. This was probably Hannahstown.

8. This was Bedford, Pennsylvania, often referred to by Shaw.

9. This was George Clymer, a signer of the Declaration of Independence and of the Constitution of 1787.

10. This was Edward Shippin V, president of the Court of Common Pleas of Philadelphia County (1784–91), and judge of the High Court of Errors and Appeals, and also a justice of the peace in 1784. He was the father-in-law of Benedict Arnold.

11. Dr. Benjamin Rush was a member of the Pennsylvania ratifying convention who helped lead the movement for the new Constitution.

12. This is now York, Pennsylvania.

13. Hunterstown was north of Gettysburg in Adams County.

14. This is Gettysburg. Some historians say that Marsh Creek settlement was the original Gettysburg and that the town became Gettysburg sometime before 1787. Others, however, say that the settlement was north of Gettys-town, so named by James Gettys, who acquired a tract and laid out the town in the late 1780s or 1790, the legislature first calling it Gettysburg in 1800 when the town charter was granted. The latter version seems more nearly correct, for a military map of the Western Quartermaster District (1784) indicates a supply depot at Marsh Creek settlement, north of the present Gettysburg.

15. This was near Hunterstown in Adams County, and no longer in existence.

16. Nottingham and Oxford are in southeastern Pennsylvania near the Maryland-Pennsylvania border.

17. Octoraro was a village on the Susquehanna River just across the border into Maryland. It was not unusual in those days to be mistaken about state lines, and it is likely that Shaw believed Octoraro was in Pennsylvania, since he made no mention of being in Maryland until he reached Charlestown.

18. London Grove Township was in the southeastern part of Chester County.

Chapter 8

1. Neither the Pennsylvania Historical Society nor the Free Library of Philadelphia was able to locate Dickworthstown.

2. White Horse, Pennsylvania, took its name from this tavern.

3. Adamstown, north of New Holland, took Shaw some distance off the regular route to Lancaster, which is west-southwest of New Holland.

4. Shaw was adding feet, not wells, and the total is incorrect.

5. Fort Washington is the site of Cincinnati, Ohio.

6. Indeed, it is "almost incredible to tell" unless Shaw meant "circumferance" instead of "diameter."

7. In "Fort Washington at Cincinnati, Ohio," the author, Robert Ralston Jones says, "As regards the water supply for the garrison, there was at least one well within the walls of the fort, this one having been dug during the summer of 1791, by one John Robert Shaw, then an enlisted soldier in the fort." The site of Fort Washington was between what is now Third, Arch, Ludlow and Broadway Streets.

8. This is now Hamilton, Ohio.

9. This was near Piqua, Ohio.

10. This is now Dry Ridge, Kentucky.

11. Elijah Craig had extensive holdings in the area (including a paper mill) near Georgetown. He laid out Georgetown.

Chapter 9

1. This was General James Wilkinson, friend of Washington and one time commander of the armies in the west, later involved in the Burr conspiracy. He owned most of Frankfort lying north of the Kentucky River—downtown Frankfort. He provided the ferry across the river and fixed its rates.

2. Some say this may have been what is now Williamstown, named for Captain William Arnold. This appears unlikely, however, since Shaw was south and west of the Kentucky River when he went to Arnold's station, whereas Williamstown is somewhat north and east of the river.

3. Jessamine County, Kentucky.

4. Hickman Creek, Jessamine County.

5. Scott's ferry house was at what was then Scott's Crossing. William Scott was governor of Kentucky from 1808 to 1812.

6. This was a few miles northeast of Lexington.

7. Maxwell Spring was a favorite spot for political rallies and debates, in which Henry Clay, John Breckinridge, George Nicholas, and others took part.

8. This was a settlement of about thirty cabins and a stockade, founded in 1779 about a mile west of Winchester, Kentucky.

9. This is in Winchester, Kentucky.

10. Thomas Hart was the father-in-law of Henry Clay.

Chapter 10

1. This is Dix River, at a point where now is Herrington Lake.

2. This was Colonel Thomas Bodley.

3. This was Dr. Ephraim McDowell, who made medical history in 1809 when he performed the first successful ovariotomy.

4. This is a reference to Horatio Nelson, victor over Napoleon at Trafalgar in 1805.

Bibliography

Books

Bowem, Catherine Drinker. *Miracle at Philadelphia*, Little, Brown & Co., 1966.

Buck, Solon, and Elizabeth Hawthorn. *Planting of Civilization in Western Pennsylvania*, University of Pittsburgh Press, 1939.

Chidsey, Donald Barr. *The Birth of the Constitution*, New York, Crown Publishers, 1966.

Clark, Thomas D. *Kentucky, Land of Contrast*, New York, Harper & Row, 1966.

Coleman, Winston. *A Bibliography of Kentucky*, n.p., 1949.

Cramer, Zedok. *Navigator: contains directions for navigating the Monongahela, Allegheny, Ohio and Mississippi Rivers*, Pittsburgh, Pa., Cramer, Spear & Eichbaum, 1810.

Espenshade, A. Howry. *Pennsylvania Place Names*, State College Studies in History and Political Science, State College, Pa., 1925.

Gregorie, Anne King. *Thomas Sumter,* Columbia, R.L. Bryan Co., 1931.

McCrady, Edward. *South Carolina in the Revolution—1776-1780*, New York, MacMillan Co., 1901.

Montgomery, Morton L. *History of Berks County, Pennsylvania*, Philadelphia, 1886.

Peter, Robert. *History of Fayette County*, O.L. Baskin & Co., Historical Publishers, Chicago, 1882.

Rankin, Hugh F. *The American Revolution*, New York, G.P. Putnam's Sons, 1964.

Roberts, Kenneth. *The Battle of Cowpens*, New York, Doubleday & Co., 1958.

Sarles, Frank B., Jr. and Charles L. Shedd. *Colonials and Patriots*, National Park Service, 1964.

Stapler, Charles B., *The History of Pioneer Lexington, 1779-1806*, Lexington, Ky., Transylvania Press, 1939.

Tousey, Lt. Col. Thomas G., United States Army. *Military History of Carlisle and Carlisle Barracks*, Dietz Press, 1939.

Wallace, Paul A.W. *Pennsylvania, Seed of a Nation*, New York, Harper & Row, 1962.

Webster's Geographical Dictionary of Names and Places, 1964 ed.

Official Documents

Statutes-at-Large of Pennsylvania, vol. 14.

American Guide Series

———— Delaware—Federal Writers Project, New York, Viking Press, 1938

———— Kentucky—Guide to the Bluegrass State, N.Y., Hastings House, 1947

———— New Jersey—Federal Writers Project, 1939

———— New York—A Guide to the Empire State, Oxford University Press, 1947

———— North Carolina—A Guide to the Old North State, Chapel Hill, University of North Carolina Press, 1939

———— Ohio—Federal Writers Project, Oxford University Press, 1948

———— Pennsylvania—A Guide to the Keystone State, University of Pennsylvania Press, 1947

———— South Carolina—A Guide to the Palmetto State, Oxford University Press, 1946

Index